German Infantry (1) 1933–40

David Westwood • Illustrated by Adam Hook

First published in Great Britain in 2002 by Osprey Publishing, Elms Court, Chapel Way, Botley, Oxford OX2 9LP, United Kingdom.
Email: info@ospreypublishing.com

ISBN 1 84176 462 0

Adam Hook has asserted his right under the Copyright, Designs and Patents Act, 1988, to be identified as the Illustrator of this Work

Editor: Tom Lowres
Design: Ken Vail Graphic Design, Cambridge, UK
Index by Alan Rutter
Originated by The Electronic Page Company, Cwmbran, UK
Printed in China through World Print Ltd.

02 03 04 05 06 10 9 8 7 6 5 4 3 2 1

FOR A CATALOGUE OF ALL BOOKS PUBLISHED BY OSPREY MILITARY AND AVIATION PLEASE CONTACT:

The Marketing Manager, Osprey Direct UK, PO Box 140, Wellingborough, Northants, NN8 2FA, United Kingdom.
Email: info@ospreydirect.co.uk

The Marketing Manager, Osprey Direct USA, c/o MBI Publishing, PO Box 1, 729 Prospect Ave, Osceola, WI 54020, USA.
Email: info@ospreydirectusa.com

www.ospreypublishing.com

Artist's note

Readers may care to note that the original paintings from which the colour plates A, B, C, D, E, and H in this book were prepared are available for private sale. All reproduction copyright whatsoever is retained by the Publishers. All enquiries should be addressed to:

Scorpio Gallery
PO Box 475
Hailsham
E. Sussex
BN27 2SL
UK

With special thanks for the creation of the digital artwork for plate G:

Encompass Graphics
4th Floor Intergen House
65/67 Western Road
Hove
E. Sussex
BN3 2JQ

And for the creation of plate F:

John Plumer
Beam Cottage
48 High Street
Topsham
Exeter
EX3 ODY

The Publishers regret that they can enter into no correspondence upon this matter.

Author's note

I am especially grateful to my friends Jason and Stephanie von Zerneck who tolerated me and my smoking for the period I was in New York researching the von Zerneck photographic collection, without which this book would have been imposssible.

All photographs are courtesy of Jason von Zerneck/Angelray books.

FRONT COVER **The German Infantryman before 1939. An Oberfeldwebel in M1935 field uniform wearing the M1935 steel helmet. (Copyright Brian Leigh Davis Collection, 544/33)**

CONTENTS

GERMAN INFANTRYMAN (1) 1933–40

INTRODUCTION – GERMANY 1919–33

The aftermath of the First World War

When the dust and arguments settled after the First World War, the victorious Allies imposed a series of restrictions on Germany in the Treaty of Versailles (June 1919). Among other things, the treaty stated that by 31 March 1920, the German army was to consist of no more than 100,000 men, of whom 4,000 were to be officers. The treaty conditions also specified the structure and organisation of this army: there were to be 21 three-battalion infantry regiments (with 21 training battalions attached), and each regiment was to have one mortar company. There were to be proportionally larger numbers of cavalry, plus seven artillery regiments of three battalions, and seven field engineer, signals, motorised and medical battalions, a total of seven divisions in all.

The German army of 34,000 officers and nearly eight million men which had fought from 1914–18 was to be reduced to insignificance, with no hope of operations larger than at corps level, and most importantly from the point of view of the French, no prospect of cross-border excursions. Furthermore, the Germans were to be prevented from forming reserves, by virtue of the restriction that men had to serve a minimum of 12 years, and officers 25 years before discharge.

The political turmoil of this period was keenly felt throughout Europe, and the heartfelt relief at the end of the slaughter was universal. Germany had removed its emperor, Kaiser Wilhelm II, at the end of the war and was struggling to find a form of government that had the power and prestige to set Germany on the way to recovery. Germany was economically and militarily bankrupt. Although American efforts to shore up what was a much weakened nation helped to some extent, political unrest was to continue in Germany until the start of the Second World War, despite the arrival of Adolf Hitler on the world stage in the 1930s.

Germany was bordered by France to the west with an army of one million. To the east was Poland, traditionally regarded as a threat by German minds, especially with its superior force of 30 infantry divisions and ten cavalry brigades. Geographically the Danzig corridor in the east separated East Prussia from the homeland, and in the Rhineland in the west, the Allies had insisted upon permanent demilitarisation as well as occupation for 15 years. To add to this and other burdens there was also the matter of reparations, a matter upon which the French were vehemently insistent.

General von Seeckt

General Hans von Seeckt became de facto Commander-in-Chief of the German army on 2 April 1920, and was faced with transforming it into the 100,000-man *Reichsheer* as specified by the Versailles treaty. He served until 7 October 1926, and, despite a personal preference for cavalry, he conceived and promulgated a doctrine which was to form the basis of German operational military thought and deed until the end of the Second World War.

Von Seeckt served on various staffs during the Great War, ending up as Chief of Staff of III Corps. For five months in 1919 he was Chief of the General Staff and spent much time immediately after the war evaluating operational concepts in which the machine gun, barbed wire, artillery and the tank had dominated. He realised that the Imperial Army was a spent force which could not fight any future war as it had done the last.

No matter what von Seeckt's political views were, his actions would affect the military world fundamentally. To avoid the tremendous losses incurred by the return to medieval siege tactics of 1914–18, he realised that military strategy had to be based on mobility. No doubt, like Field Marshal Haig, he had longed to loose the cavalry into the enemy's rear after a breakthrough of the front-line enemy trenches. More perceptively, he also saw that such breakthroughs were not easily achieved once the enemy had time to dig in and fortify. He had, however, noted the successes of the *Sturmgruppen* who had made such progress in 1918. What he emphasised was that such breakthroughs had to be supplied, and then resupplied with men, weapons, food and all the other prerequisites of warfare.

The size of the new army was always a consideration, but his plan was that the army would enlarge itself as soon as it could. The political situation was not suitable until 1933. The essence of his teaching was that 'tactics depend upon co-operation between arms' and that the next war would be one 'of manoeuvre'.

Unlike many staff officers, von Seeckt was well travelled and had been educated at a secondary school in Strasbourg rather than in a military school, which probably endowed him with more flexibility of mind than the traditional unbending military education. His work from 1920–26 resulted in the publication of a pamphlet, *Führung und Gefecht* ('Command in Battle'), which emphasised the importance of movement in battle. He wanted an army which was only big enough to counter a surprise enemy attack. The real strength of this new army would lie in its mobility which would be provided by a large contingent of cavalry, physically well-conditioned infantry, and a full complement of motorised or mechanised units, machine guns and artillery. Of course the men of the Reichswehr were already battle-hardened, experienced fighters. All he had to do was train them to exploit their mobility.

Von Seeckt's work was of such importance that, from 1923, the German army began to base its training and exercises on his published theories, and although the army had very few men to put on the ground in exercises, the basic elements of his ideas became fundamental to German strategic and tactical thinking. The emphasis was rapid reaction to new events, together with a preparedness for decisive action against the enemy. Exercises and manoeuvres from 1923 to 1926 showed how the concept of this war of movement was also becoming standard thinking in the German army right down to section level.

Although von Seeckt had retired by 1933 when Hitler and the NSDAP came to power, his legacy to the German army had not been lost.

Hitler was elected on 30 January 1933, under the critical eye of Field Marshal von Hindenburg. Hitler intended to enlarge the army to further his expansionist aims in Europe, and the army was naturally delighted. Senior officers believed Hitler could be controlled: nothing, however, could have been further from the truth.

The military districts (*Wehrkreise*)

Germany had been divided into military districts for recruitment purposes since before the First World War. Each district recruited and trained the men for the army, and within each district there were the relevant corps headquarters, barracks and training areas needed for the Reichswehr. On Hitler's accession he made it quite plain that the army was to expand from the original seven divisions to a total of 36 divisions in 13 corps. The army's initial reaction was one of total surprise, as they contemplated the sheer logistical problems of such enormous expansion. However, they were delighted to be free of the restrictions imposed by the Treaty of Versailles, with the army assuming an honourable position within German society once again.

The Military Districts (*Wehrkreise*) in Germany 1939. The towns were the administrative centres of their respective areas.

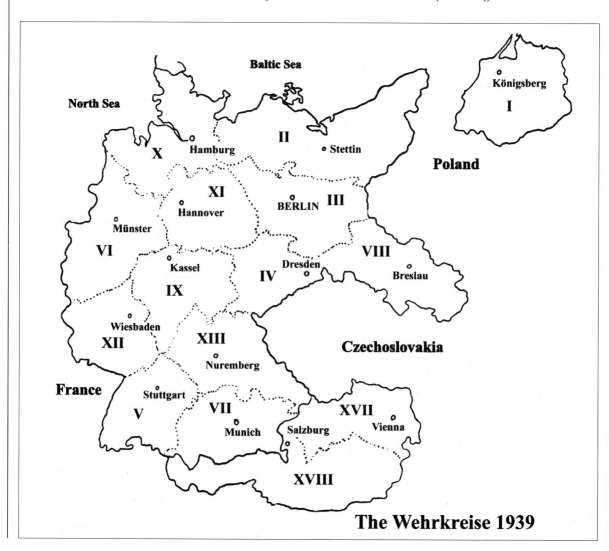

The Wehrkreise 1939

Every German male was to be liable to serve in the armed forces, although this had been forbidden by the Versailles treaty. On 16 March 1935 Hitler promulgated the 'Law for the expansion of the German Armed Forces' which reinstated the system, and increased the army to 36 divisions. On 21 May 1935 a second law defined the duty to serve in the Armed Forces (or the *Wehrmacht* as they were now known), noting very few exceptions. Although Hitler was still establishing the power base of the NSDAP, his relationship with the army was strengthened by these laws, for it meant that at long last, the small, professional army created and trained under von Seeckt would now have new men to train and a much greater standing in society at home and in the military world at large.

From 2 August 1934, all German soldiers swore the following oath: 'I swear by God this holy oath: that I will always be unconditionally obedient to Adolf Hitler, Leader of the German Reich and people, Supreme Commander of the Wehrmacht, and, as a valiant soldier I am prepared to lay down my life at any time for this oath.'

RECRUITMENT AND TRAINING

This new, much enlarged army needed recruits. The *Wehrkreise* (13 in 1933) were ordered to use the registration lists held by the police (listing all German nationals, their addresses and ages, as well as foreigners and Jews) to start calling up all men who had reached their 20th year. The civil and military authorities worked independently and jointly to ensure that this process was seamlessly incorporated into German life, aided by the constantly broadcast reminder that the profession of the German soldier was one of honour. Propaganda extolled the life of the soldier: increasingly civilians were trained (from childhood onwards) in military ways.

The all-pervading effect of the Nazi Party was especially felt in the newly created Hitler Youth (*Hitlerjugend*) and the German Labour Service (*Reichsarbeitsdienst*). No one of the relevant age could avoid becoming a member and both organisations (and many others with perhaps the single exception of the League of Young German Women, *Bund Deutscher Mädel*) were paramilitary in ethos. Training was based on foot drill, map reading, field craft and weapon training (with small bore weapons). The German Labour Service served as the middle stage for all German men between the Hitler Youth and the armed forces. Many men had good reason to remember their efforts on the Labour Service when they joined the army, because the training they had already undergone prepared them both physically and mentally for army training. When they arrived at their army depots, however, they were reminded constantly by their instructors that 'we did not know how to march, we did not even know how to walk'.

Every individual who was liable to serve in the army was warned in the summer of his call-up year, receiving a letter containing the basic details of where he was to report. A second letter in September then told him when to report, and what papers he needed to bring: his membership cards and records of service in the Hitler Youth and the Labour Service were specified as important documents.

New recruits at their first moment at 30 Infantry Regiment barracks, 1934.

The new barracks were purpose-built and often included double-glazing and central heating.

The training depots

Training depots had a deserved reputation for harshness, but the aim of the training was dictated by the experiences of the First World War. Most of the NCOs who were training the recruits were veterans of the trenches and knew only too well that men did not fight well if they were tired, hungry, cold, wet or demoralised. Furthermore, von Seeckt's demands that this professional army must be mobile meant that men had to be ready at all times, not only when they were well fed and rested. So, the NCOs pushed the trainees to breaking point. Their motto was simple: 'Sweat saves blood' (*'Schweiß spart Blut'*).

Recruits faced 16 weeks of what was probably the most effective basic training provided by any army of the time. Already fuelled by the incessant propaganda from the Party and the army, men were installed in barracks with a fervour to serve rarely seen in any army. In no time they were writing home to say 'I have a brand-new uniform ... and am very proud of my appearance ... I learn some military songs.'

Basic training was designed to turn raw recruits into soldiers who would obey. However, von Seeckt's influence was still felt, and every German soldier was trained to act upon his own initiative if circumstances demanded it. The German army was not inclined to Napoleon's dictum that every man has a marshal's baton in his knapsack, but rather, that every man could and should act one rank (at least) higher up than his actual appointment.

The recruits were constantly told that their oath was the very essence of their lives and that, 'The honour of soldiers lies in their unconditional personal commitment to their people and nation, even unto death.'

The aim of basic training

Depot training was planned meticulously with every hour of the day used to good purpose. It started by putting the men into uniform, training them in drilling together on the square, instructing them in how to wear their various uniforms, how to keep them clean, and how to stay fit and well. Further training with rifle, pistol, grenade, bayonet, submachine gun and machine gun, together with constant field exercises, combined to produce efficient soldiers.

They also learned map-reading, military writing and reporting, field craft, range estimation, target description and the various aspects of the infantry land battle. They were shown films on weapons and the effect of their fire, on movement across country, anti-aircraft protection, anti-tank operations and camouflage. They were taught to dig trenches for themselves, and later for support weapons.

The result was intended to be a soldier who was capable of existing within his section in the land battle, and of fighting effectively. He was expected to be smart, respectful to seniors, and a source of pride to his parents and neighbours. After 16 weeks he passed out and went on to more practical training with greater insight into the future method of all-arms warfare, based initially at company, and later at battalion and regimental level.

A range day, 1936. This particularly interesting photograph shows a platoon undergoing instruction. To the left rear, the riflemen are being taught by a corporal. The range officer is seated on the motorcycle and the platoon commander is on the mudguard. In the foreground, selected men are being evaluated for ability with the MG 34, and one recruit is in the process of clearing the weapon after firing under the watchful eyes of three NCOs. The line of soldiers by the company clerk's table are waiting their turn.

The training programme

When recruits first arrived to muster with 30 Infantry Regiment, they came from the local area around Görlitz, and already knew some members of their battalion, perhaps even of the regiment. Nevertheless, friendship was limited to their immediate fellows in the first 16 weeks of training. They were allocated rooms on the basis of one per section (*Korporalschaft*), and they met their section commander, a lance corporal (*Gefreiter*) whom they would learn to fear and respect when on duty.

The platoon sergeant (*Feldwebel*), with whom they would have more to do later on in their course, and their platoon commander made brief appearances, the officer to give them a lecture on the German army and its place in German society. They were now officially banned from having any political affiliations whatsoever, which meant that the members of the NSDAP had to make friends (like it or not) with non-Party members.

The training programme depended to an extent on the depot at which the soldiers were trained. Some depots and training areas had a reputation for extremes of discipline bordering on the sadistic; others were less intensive, but just as instructive. Men who were to join 30 Infantry Regiment, part of 18 Infantry Division, were first assembled in the autumn of the year at Görlitz in eastern Germany, not far from the Polish - German - Czech border junction.

The room allotted to each section was theirs for 16 weeks, and so was its cleanliness. They were then issued with a range of personal uniform equipment, given a severe haircut, and finally fed at around six in the evening. After the meal they received their first ideological lecture on the German army, its traditions and ethos, and their regiment. They were also shown how to wear their uniforms, and warned to pack up all civilian clothing for posting back home the next day. They were now soldiers, and subject to military discipline; they were also instructed on saluting in and out of doors, and reminded that respect was due to any member of the German army senior to them – which meant almost everyone they met.

The training day

This began at 5 am when the men were often literally thrown out of their beds by the corporals and soldiers responsible for barracks training. The men then had to strip their beds, tidy their lockers, wash, shave and dress before breakfast. Many mornings would also include runs of increasing distance and speed before ablutions and dressing in uniform. On some days the men were writing home: 'Early in the morning at 4 am out of our beds for a long cross-country run', and 'We have to get up at five o'clock every morning.'

Breakfast of coffee and bread followed at 6.45 am, so for 15 minutes the men were relatively free to eat. Often this meal was not available, however, especially if the men were on exercise or drilling to correct the previous day's errors. Recruits learned very quickly that 'hunger, tiredness and personal discomfort were of little consequence', and that they had to be ready for anything at any time. The soundness of this training was proved time and again, even in the later war years, when the resilience and stamina of ordinary German soldiers was remarked on by all those who fought against them. One soldier wrote, 'In action later on, we realised time and again how valuable this training had been for us. "Sweat saves blood", that was a truism that was often confirmed later. We didn't know it yet though, so we cursed and swore at everything and everyone.'

Lectures were part of the day (and woe betide anyone who slumped in his seat, or worse, fell asleep). Topics ranged from the initial lectures on the duties of the soldier to his comrades in arms, to the soldier and the state, and who was who in the Nazi hierarchy. Little except the very basics of battle training was included in lectures, the German method being to show men in the field what they should do in the field.

Each day was divided into morning and afternoon training, and a typical morning might include a lecture and drill on the square. The afternoon might have been devoted to an hour of physical training, training on the light machine gun and shooting practice. Shooting was fundamental to training and one soldier described it, 'So, it's on to the firing range, which itself is a few miles distant. There are at least a thousand men, and the firing is non-stop.' The main meal, lunch (*Mittagessen*), when it was eaten, was served at 12.30 pm, giving the men another few moments of peace, although sometimes the recruits found that 'Lunch here is at eleven. You arrived late, so, it's time for drill.'

At 1.30 pm, no matter what else they were doing in the afternoon, all the recruits were assembled on the square, inspected and given any notices relevant to them. This parade was taken initially by the platoon sergeants, then at a later stage of training by the company sergeant major, and later still by platoon commanders, then the company adjutant and the company

In barracks much time was spent cleaning personal equipment and weapons. The man on the right is putting the final touches to his rifle before inspection, 1936.

commander. The men met their officers infrequently during training for the reason that they would be commanded by others in battle, and had to learn to survive at section and platoon level first, without the comforting presence of an officer.

Evenings were spent cleaning uniforms and kit, rifles, machine guns, and then the room itself. The evening meal (*Abendbrot*) was taken at 6.30 pm, and further activities could stretch the working day well into the dark, and later in training, throughout the night.

Barracks training
Personal clothing and equipment
The German army distinguished between barracks training and field training; field training included drill on the square, as well as field craft, weapon training, map reading and the other skills required for survival in the

field. Barracks training involved personal cleanliness (which was heavily stressed), as well as weapon cleaning, and the inevitable chores of floor polishing, bed making and general household duties with which all armies concern themselves. Barracks training, however, created the bonds of friendship in sections that lasted into battle.

The recruits to 30 IR were issued with everything needed to perform their many duties in the appropriate dress. The table shows the various dress orders that recruits were expected to wear. Needless to say, it was every man's own responsibility to keep himself and all his equipment clean and in a good state of repair. Reissues of clothing and equipment were made, but in the interim only damage due to training or exercise would warrant special replacement of any item.

Two members of an MG team are seen cleaning the weapon under the supervision of the gun commander in 1938. The man on the left is cleaning a two-barrel spare barrel container. The man in the centre works on the breech mechanism of the gun, which has its bipod mounted in the mid-position. On the bench in the foreground is an anti-aircraft tripod, or *Dreibein*.

Cards after the evening meal, 1936. As training intensified, spare time began to disappear.

German army dress regulations

1. Battle Dress (all troops)
- Steel helmet (alternatively, side hat when not in the battle zone)
- Field jacket and collar
- Shoulder straps (attached to belt)
- Long trousers
- Boots
- Gloves
- Greatcoat
- Pack
- Shelter quarter and lining
- Belt
- Bread bag
- Water bottle and cup
- Gas mask
- Cartridge pouches and sling for ammunition boxes
- Kit bag (carried in company wagon)
- Entrenching tool
- Personal weapon

NCOs and others with need of the following:
- Spurs
- Map case
- Whistle
- Binoculars
- Pistol
- Medals
- Cyclist's cape

2. Parade dress
- Steel helmet
- Field or Dress jacket and collar
- Shoulder straps (attached to belt)
- Long trousers
- Boots
- Belt
- Bayonet (with *Troddel* when authorised - a *Troddel* was a bayonet adornment of silk with a wound tassel similar to a sword knot. Issued to permanent staff of a training or operational unit)
- Full size medals
- Cartridge pouches
- Pack with rolled greatcoat

If so ordered:
- Rolled shelter half (over greatcoat on pack)
- Coat
- Gloves (always worn by NCOs)

3. Service dress
- Either side hat or helmet
- Field or Dress jacket and collar
- Tie
- Gloves
- Long trousers
- Boots
- Spurs
- Belt
- Bayonet (or pistol)
- Medals

NCOs and others when appropriate
- Whistle
- Binoculars
- Coat
- Pack
- Cartridge pouches

4. Formal barracks wear
- Side hat
- Field or Dress jacket and collar
- Long trousers
- Boots
- Belt
- Bayonet (with *Troddel* for NCOs)
- Medals

NCOs only
- Gloves

5. Walking-out dress
- Peaked cap
- Field jacket
- Long trousers
- (Coat)
- Gloves
- Shoes
- Belt
- Bayonet
- Medals

6. Sports wear
- Sports shirt
- Sports shorts
- Running shoes
- (Swimming costume)

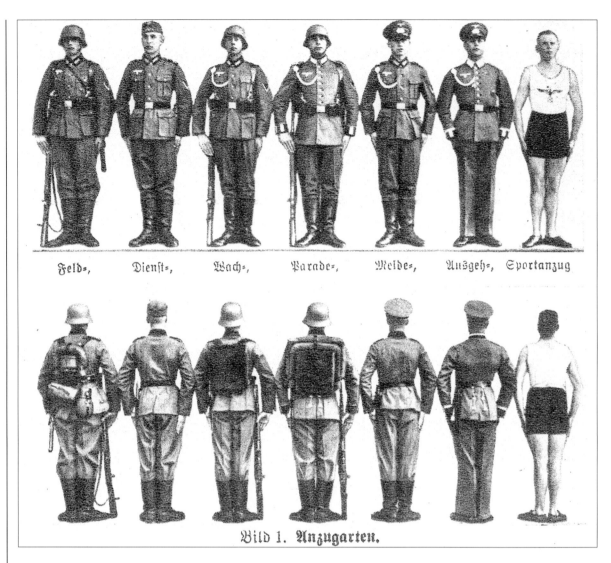

Feld=,   Dienſt=,   Wach=,   Parade=,   Melde=,   Ausgeh=,   Sportanzug

Bild 1. Anzugarten.

An original page from Reibert showing the different dress and uniforms of the German Army 1939.

Boots had to be carefully looked after, for damaged or ill-fitting boots could cause a man to drop out from the line of march, possibly with dire consequences. Certainly, foot damage caused by badly fitting boots was a serious offence.

Recruits also had to strip back their beds every morning to allow them to air. Hot, sweaty soldiers have never been renowned for their personal hygiene, especially if they are also tired, and a sweat-soaked bed needed fresh air before it was remade in the early afternoon before roll-call.

Lockers, too, were subject to the basic rule of tidiness, although the German army at this time did not make a fetish of 'spit and polish' like some other armies. Cleanliness and tidiness were paramount, but a glass-like shine on boots, or beds squared away to the millimetre, was not demanded as a general rule.

The uniform of the day for trainees was perhaps the most awkward that could be chosen, for it was white. Once washed many times it would age to a yellow/grey colour, but it was difficult to keep clean enough for inspections. Ankle boots, belt and side hat completed the trainees'

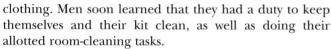

clothing. Men soon learned that they had a duty to keep themselves and their kit clean, as well as doing their allotted room-cleaning tasks.

Punishment for error was swift and effective, almost always involving physically demanding tasks which made uniforms and equipment even dirtier, thus compounding the offence. Interestingly, all such punishments were also regarded as training events, and so polishing dustbins and painting grass green were not among the prescribed sanctions. Instead, men would be made to go on a long run in full field gear, or made to practise field movements, especially crawling through muddy sumps and wading through streams and rivers. On some occasions however the punishment was physically very demanding. One soldier wrote: 'I had to put on the punishment pack … which weighed nearly eighty pounds … After two hours my helmet was burning hot from the sun, and by the end I needed all my willpower to keep my knees from buckling … I learned that a good soldier does not cross the barracks square with his hands in his pockets.'

ABOVE LEFT **Outside a barrack block a group of instructors (in field uniform) and their students (in fatigue uniform and short boots) pause for a group photograph. The recruits are nearing the end of their initial 16 weeks training.**

ABOVE RIGHT **Inspection of one section's personal torches and gas masks, 1938.**

Field training
Foot drill and rifle drill

One way to show recruits the meaning of obedience is firm training in foot and rifle drill. Many hours were spent on the square during the 16 weeks of training (an average of 30 periods per week, which included muster parades and parades prior to meals). However, rifle drill in the German army was not limited to parade handling: it also included tactical handling – loading, unloading, making safe, cleaning and tactical handling.

The role of the rifleman was not the same as in other European armies of the time: in the German army the rifleman was in battle to carry out the final assault on the enemy after the machine gun had won the fire fight. Other European armies regarded the rifleman as the heart of the infantry because he carried a bayonet. Other armies regarded machine guns as support, not main weapons.

Weapons and weapon training

Recruits were initially issued the Gewehr 98 rifle, which was designed and made by the Mauser Company at Oberndorf in the Neckar Valley. Experience in the First World War had shown that it was too long for practical purposes, and so it was shortened and improved with a turned bolt, becoming the Kar 98k, the weapon that served throughout the period 1933–45.

It was a 7.92 mm (0.312 in.) calibre weapon. weighing 3.89 kg (8 lb 9 oz). The *k* at the end of its title denoted that it was a shorter version of the original (40.4 cm, compared with 49.6 cm). The ballistics of the cartridge had also been improved, and the new rifle fired a cartridge with a muzzle velocity of 762 mps.

The weapon had a staggered five-round magazine, barleycorn sights, and was still equipped with a cleaning/ram rod, which was to prove extremely effective in the winter in Russia. It was later partly superseded by semi-automatic weapons.

One aspect of training that was common to every army (then and now) was rifle cleaning. Whether or not the weapon had been fired, it had to be carefully maintained every day. This meant wiping off any dirt from the weapon, pulling the barrel through and lightly oiling it and the bolt and breech, magazine follower and spring and the safety mechanism and sights.

Throughout the 16-week training a total of 398 instructional periods were devoted to rifle handling and drill on the square, and 234 periods on shooting, meaning that for the rifle alone, each recruit averaged 40 sessions a week. He fired over 300 rounds on the range in this period.

Every soldier also carried a bayonet on his left hip. This was sometimes of limited value, but was handy as a fighting knife (and for opening tins), and was never dispensed with. The proliferation of automatic weapons such as submachine guns, machine guns and hand grenades, limited combat use of the bayonet in the Second World War. Submachine guns were better for close-quarter fighting, machine guns reached out so far on the battlefield that they often precluded hand-to-hand combat; the grenade was particularly effective in house-clearing work, where the bayonet imposed restrictions on the use of the rifle. In Russia, however, close-combat was the norm in many

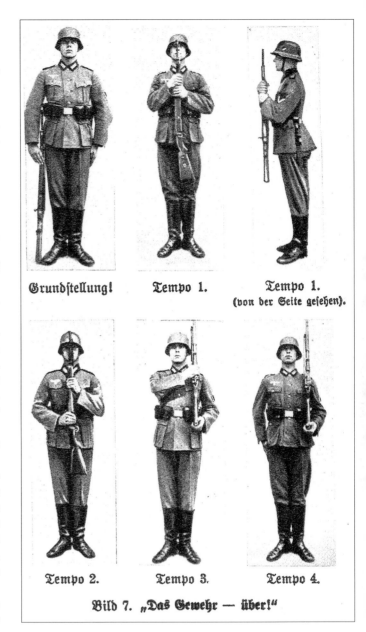

Grundstellung!   Tempo 1.   Tempo 1.
(von der Seite gesehen).

Tempo 2.   Tempo 3.   Tempo 4.

Bild 7. „Das Gewehr — über!"

Another original Reibert page, showing the movements for shoulder arms drill.

situations, and as long as the bayonet did not interfere with movement, it was fixed and used.

The bayonet had to be cared for as much as the rifle, and so it was wiped clean with a slightly oily rag every day, and no rust was to appear at any time.

The light machine gun.

The German army based its infantry sections on the firepower of the machine gun. The machine gun had proved its value in both defence and attack during the First World War, and von Seeckt recommended that every infantry section should consist of a machine gun to win local fire fights, with a number of riflemen acting as support for the machine gun in defence, and as the assault party in the attack. This principle meant that every section now had the firepower of a platoon of riflemen (at least), and was able to lay down defensive, interdictory or suppressing fire as the situation required.

The first machine guns of the Reichswehr were extremely heavy and cumbersome. The MG 15 (or Maxim 08) was a water-cooled gun weighing 19.28 kg (42.5 lb). The tripod was similarly heavy. The weapon was rifle calibre, but fired its ammunition from a fabric belt. The gun served well in the fixed positions of the First World War, but was eventually eliminated because it was too awkward to be moved quickly.

Carrying water to refill the gun's cooling water jacket was burdensome and if water supplies were limited the gun was prone to overheat, so the German army went over to air-cooled weapons. Incidentally, the MG 08 and the later MG 08/15 were still on issue in 1940 to second-line divisions, and they are to be seen in operation in the photographs in this book.

Designed around the MG 18 of the First World War, the MG 13 was a lighter section weapon, bipod-mounted, air-cooled, and fed by a magazine. However, it was only used as a training weapon, for the next generation of machine gun was on the drawing boards in the early 1930s: the MG 34.

The MG 34 was a belt-fed light machine gun which was air-cooled and could be tripod-mounted. The Germans had decided that they would combine many roles into one weapon, and this machine gun was an excellent design. It was useful to infantry in both defence and attack, could double as an anti-aircraft local defence weapon, or could be made into a sustained fire medium machine gun with no modification to the weapon itself. With some modification, it also served as a tank-mounted local defence weapon.

The ammunition for the gun (of rifle calibre) was supplied either by 50-round belt or 75-round drum. Later drums carried 150 rounds, and were issued in pairs in a carrier. The belt was a fixed-link design, and

Machine guns were of prime importance to the German army and this posed photograph of 1935 shows an infantryman behind a Browning 0.30in. machine gun of First World War vintage.

could be reloaded from cartridge boxes very quickly. The ammunition carriers for the gun both carried two boxes of ammunition, each containing at least 294 rounds. Every gunner carried a tool and spares wallet on his belt, which contained, among other useful items, some belt starters for the gun. These allowed linked belts to be fed into the gun with the top cover closed, giving the gunner more flexibility. Linked belts could also be joined to make more cartridges available, a feature that was particularly valuable in the face of mass attacks such as those launched by the Russians in reaction to Operation Barbarossa.

A 1938 machine gun platoon poses with their MG 34s on the tripods which were used for sustained fire. From left to right: the platoon wagon driver, the platoon commander, and behind the left gun, six gunners (including the gun commander). A further six gunners are behind the right gun, with the range taker and his range finder in front of the two guns. The men either side of the range taker and the man on the extreme right are replacements.

Each infantry section was divided into a machine gun group and an assault (rifle) group. The machine gun was regarded as the firepower of the section, and to ensure sustained use, the group had a gunner (with the gun itself) who was supported by two ammunition carriers, one of whom carried the spare barrel (later two spare barrels) for the gun. Barrel changing was quite simple, involving only a few seconds and the use of a protective pad against the heat in the old barrel. Barrel changes were recommended after every 250 rounds of battle use.

The MG 34 was the first real general purpose machine gun, and it was a superb piece of engineering. Unfortunately this was its undoing, for the strict engineering processes required for its manufacture also made it prone to stoppages, and it was eventually replaced to a large extent by the MG 42. However, the MG 34 was a valuable weapon. The rate of fire was such that in a good gunner's hands the gun could easily lay down enough fire to prevent an enemy manoeuvring close to the Germans, and in defence, could cut an attacking force to pieces.

All recruits received initial training on the weapon, but anyone who showed aptitude for the gun was given extra training in all its aspects. No doubt this was sometimes regarded as a curse by those chosen, for they now had extra duties to perform, and they had to carry the gun and its ammunition in the field. Initial training totalled 68 hours, including six hours on the range.

Type 24 hand grenade

In the First World War the German army had probably the most effective hand grenade of the era, which became the Type 24 hand grenade and was still on issue in 1935. Its long handle allowed it to be thrown far further, and with greater accuracy, than any contemporary grenade. Its effect was well known (and was later augmented with a fragmentation sleeve), and it is seen in many contemporary photographs (although the majority are posed). The weapon was so simple to use that only three hours were needed to make recruits basically proficient in its use.

The Pistole 08 (or Luger)

This famous weapon was issued to all machine gunners as a personal weapon, as well as to vehicle drivers, horse handlers and other personnel whose jobs precluded them from carrying a rifle. The design by Hugo Borchardt and George Luger was extremely interesting, but gave it no special military characteristics. Like all pistols (including the later Walther P38) it was a very short range, desperation weapon which was carried because it was issued rather than from choice. Six hours training time was allotted to the weapon.

The submachine gun

The Germans observed in the First World War that many weapons used in trench warfare were standard issue, and were basically too long and cumbersome to be used in enclosed spaces such as trenches and buildings. Having seen some early Russian submachine guns, they adopted the MP 38 as a section commander's weapon, and devoted some training periods to it. It was excellent at close ranges for putting a lot of fire on a target, and it was extremely simple to use, strip and clean. Furthermore, it used the standard 9 mm pistol cartridge already issued for the Pistole 08 and later the P38. Ten hours training were allotted to this weapon.

The infantry mortar

This weapon was issued to every platoon, as it was intended for short-range support. It was 5 cm calibre, and fired high explosive (HE), smoke and illumination bombs. All infantry were trained in its use, but in basic training only familiarity training was given (and see Plate 4).

The role of the mortar was to give area support to attacking infantry with its HE bombs, and also to provide cover for movement with smoke bombs. It also fired illumination bombs equipped with a delaying parachute, which were of great value during night defensive operations. Although the HE bomb was only of limited effect, it had a good effect on morale, and the 5 cm mortar continued in platoon use for many years.

There was one limitation to its use, however. The first models had an extremely complex levelling mechanism (based on that used with heavier mortars) which delayed action times for the mortar team. This was later eradicated and the 5 cm mortar served well as the platoon howitzer.

Musketry

Rifle shooting practice began without ammunition, using tripods and an aiming disk. The first few shots were fired at short range. As soon as the best shots in each section were recognised, these men were instructed intensively on the light machine gun (naturally in addition to their other tasks). At least five hours a week were devoted to training on the light machine gun, which included loading, unloading, stoppages, aiming techniques and fire plans. As the

A platoon light mortar team on exercise. The mortar itself is in front of the layer (the man on the left), and his loader to his right. An open box of 5 cm mortar bombs can be seen to the right of the loader's right leg. (1937)

weeks went by, the machine gun section and the rifle section were slowly integrated into their battle sections.

Training in musketry went on throughout the soldier's life in the German army, and his marksmanship (or otherwise) was under constant review. Thus training began, with 'dry' aiming (no cartridge in the weapon) under the strict supervision of an NCO. Once he had learned the basics of holding and aiming his rifle properly, the soldier progressed to the training tables. Each trainee fired a few rounds in different positions from the training tables, with an NCO constantly at his side to correct faults and to improve technique.

The first shooting position was lying down with the rifle supported, then he practised shooting while sitting. Trainees progressed to unsupported firing lying, kneeling, sitting and (most difficult of all) standing. Every round fired was recorded by the company clerk, and the platoon NCOs were always willing to increase the required training if necessary. The essence of the training was to make every recruit utterly familiar with his rifle and its capabilities on the range. Field firing with live ammunition came later, but only when the trainee was well versed in safety procedures and was known to be able to exercise common sense.

Other training

Once the basics of self-organisation were instilled into the recruits they were able to go on to certain more advanced aspects of their training.

Ballistics

German soldiers were instructed in the classroom on the basic technical aspects of ballistics, learning about the components of their rifle and the cartridge it fired. They learnt about which type of cartridge they were firing, and what its purpose was. The German army used a standard 7.92 mm rimless rifle and machine gun cartridge, which had a number of bullets. The basic infantry cartridge was the *sS* cartridge, a simple lead-cored, fully jacketed round. It also had the *SmK* round, which was cored with steel beneath a lead tip, again fully jacketed.

A third type of round was the *SmKL'spur*, a cored tracer round whose trajectory was similar to that of standard ammunition. This was particularly important in night firing, as it followed the same trajectory as the invisible non-tracer rounds which were also being fired. A fourth type was the incendiary bullet, which was filled with phosphorus.

Further ballistics training went into some detail about mortar and artillery shells.

Map reading

Each individual German infantryman had to be able to use a map. This was a reflection of the basic concept that every man had to be able to do the job of his commander, no matter what their respective ranks. He was trained in the use of the compass and square, and was able to give eight-figure grid references, to assess dead ground from a map (by drawing a section), and how to orient his map and navigate with it. Troops also had to be able to recognise and name land forms, and to evaluate the cover that terrain might afford them in attack and defence. They were taught to do this partly by map reading and partly by practical exercise.

To learn the trade of his superior NCOs, the recruit had to be able to work out the best route for crossing country both in attack and defence. He could get some help from the map, but frequent practical exercises drove home the lesson that cover is essential when moving, whether it is by fire or by using ground and artificial structures to remain concealed from the enemy. This concealment had two aims: to reduce casualties and to make every attempt at hiding movement from the enemy.

Range estimation

This skill was important, for although at battalion level the machine gun company had a portable range-finder, it was important for every soldier to be able to estimate range so that effective fire orders could be given. Lectures in ballistics covered the effective beaten zone of bullets at the end of their trajectory, so all infantrymen were aware of the need to estimate ranges accurately so that the effective beaten zone was where it needed to be – on top of the enemy.

Mortar and artillery fire control

All infantry were given basic instruction in issuing fire orders to mortar teams at battalion level and above, and to the regimental artillery. When the artillery observation officer was not on site, any infantry unit could call for fire from the regimental guns, in addition to fixed 'SOS' fire tasks. The co-operation between infantry in the line and mortars and artillery was good at all times, meaning that fire support was usually effective and timely.

Infantry/tank co-operation

The men were introduced to mock tanks during their 16 weeks training, until such time as the real thing was available. Very few of the infantry regiments were given any in-depth familiarisation with the new weapon, as the Panzer divisions were expected to work on their own, with the infantry coming up behind to consolidate their territorial gains. Not enough thought or effort had gone into motorising the infantry, and the German army began to suffer as the war went on; tanks unprotected by infantry are vulnerable to anti-tank weapons, and infantry on their own cannot break through well-defended front lines.

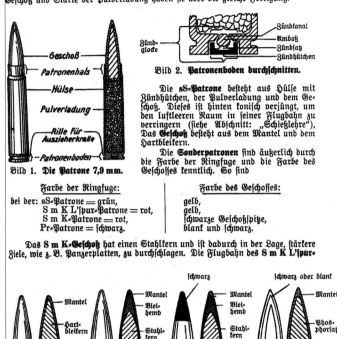

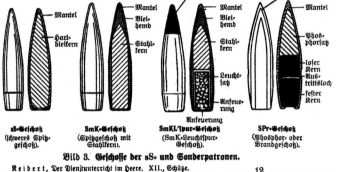

An original page from Reibert's infantry training handbook, dealing with types of ammunintion and bullets.

Infantry-tank co-operation training. This early 1934 photograph shows two infantry sections with a mock tank. The turret is wood, and is mounted on a lorry chassis. The tank 'commander' is also probably a member of the infantry regiment as he has no tank insignia on his uniform.

Company and regimental support weapons

All trainees were given lectures and practical demonstrations in the use and effect of the heavy machine gun in battle. They were lectured on the artillery support available to every unit within the regiment from the artillery battalion, as well as the support available from the heavy company with its 8 cm mortars (see colour plate E). Those who showed a particular aptitude with a specific heavy weapon could expect further training with it, and might be transferred to the relevant platoon when capable of carrying out the duties required to fight with the weapon.

The German infantry regiment in 1939

The German infantry regiment was intended to be tactically self-sufficient in operations against an enemy battalion, based on a three-to-one superiority in the attack. As the organisation chart shows, it had enough firepower in both offence and defence to defeat any enemy of that strength. Practically, the firepower was often enough to defeat larger units in both roles, for German defence tactics were dependent upon the machine guns of the infantry, in addition to the artillery and mortars at regimental level.

The chart shows that the regiment was able to use its mounted platoon for reconnaissance tasks, its infantry element for operations in attack and defence, and could support those operations with its heavy weapons at company, battalion and regimental level. The German infantry regiment was a small reflection of the division, of which it was a component. Each division (pre-war) had nine infantry regiments, together with supporting arms and services.

Winter training, 1937. Here a heavy MG 34 is mounted on its tripod with the dial sight fitted. The gun commander is on the right, with an ammunition man holding the belt, whilst the gunner is behind the gun. A further ammunition man stands at the rear.

The German Infantry Regiment (pre-war)

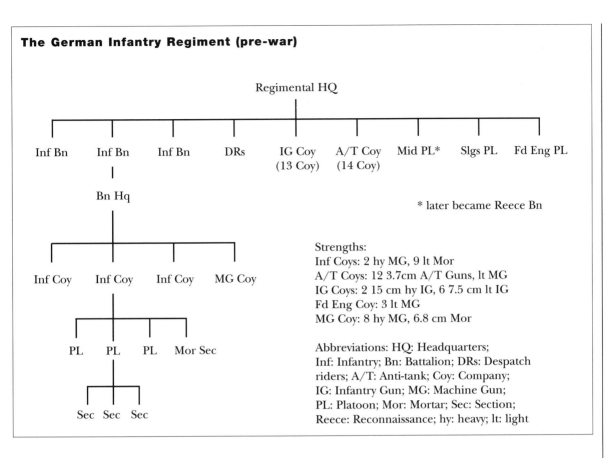

```
                          Regimental HQ
                               |
  ┌──────┬──────┬──────┬──────┼──────┬──────┬──────┬──────┐
Inf Bn  Inf Bn  Inf Bn  DRs  IG Coy  A/T Coy  Mid PL*  Slgs PL  Fd Eng PL
          |                  (13 Coy) (14 Coy)
        Bn Hq
          |
  ┌──────┬──────┬──────┐
Inf Coy Inf Coy Inf Coy MG Coy
          |
   ┌──────┬──────┬──────┐
  PL     PL     PL    Mor Sec
          |
      ┌────┬────┐
     Sec  Sec  Sec
```

* later became Reece Bn

Strengths:
Inf Coys: 2 hy MG, 9 lt Mor
A/T Coys: 12 3.7cm A/T Guns, lt MG
IG Coys: 2 15 cm hy IG, 6 7.5 cm lt IG
Fd Eng Coy: 3 lt MG
MG Coy: 8 hy MG, 6.8 cm Mor

Abbreviations: HQ: Headquarters;
Inf: Infantry; Bn: Battalion; DRs: Despatch
riders; A/T: Anti-tank; Coy: Company;
IG: Infantry Gun; MG: Machine Gun;
PL: Platoon; Mor: Mortar; Sec: Section;
Reece: Reconnaissance; hy: heavy; lt: light

ABOVE **The organisation of a German Infantry Regiment in 1939.**

LEFT **Anti-tank range practice, 1938. The reconnaissance battalion heavy company included a platoon of 37 mm anti-tank guns (three guns). Here the anti-tank guns are being used for range practice in the second stage of training. In the foreground the gun layer (kneeling, facing the target) under the gun commander (standing with field glasses) fires the gun, whilst the loader (on the far side of the gun, also kneeling) keeps the weapon ready for firing. Other gun numbers are just behind the commander, and the fifth member of the team is getting more ammunition from the boxes to the rear of the gun.**

German regiments were as cohesive as their British counterparts, and there was enormous pride in the activities of one's regiment. However, German soldiers were always kept informed of the intentions not only of their battalion and regiment, but also of the division, which attracted as much loyalty as the regiment.

The battalion telephone exchange on an exercise, 1937. Up to battalion level, most of the signals were sent by runner. The infantry were always short of radio sets, and came to rely on telephones heavily. Previously the German army had also used pigeons and heliograph, as well as telephones.

Relaxation in training, 1937 – a rare moment given the punishing schedule. The men have erected a standard field tent from shelter quarters. They are all wearing the standard issue greatcoat.

The OrBat of the regiment also shows the support elements at each level. The machine gun company in each battalion had four pairs of heavy machine guns and six medium mortars. The heavy machine guns were MG 34s with tripod mounts and dial sighting systems, enabling them to undertake indirect fire tasks. By using map plotting and aiming stakes, the machine guns could be aligned with a primary, long range and unseen, target onto which fire could be directed as required. Further targets could then be plotted at will and recorded on a master plot by the section or company commander. All the gunners had to do was lay out guide stakes for pre-planned fire tasks, and simply aim the dial sight at them, adjusting elevation and deflection as necessary.

The main task for the heavy machine guns was shooting in an attack. Individual section guns were on the move during infantry attacks, and the Germans reasoned that more machine gun support constantly firing on the *Schwerpunkt* (the main attack point where maximum effort was concentrated for penetration of the front line) of the attack would be of great value. This led to the formation of machine gun companies, tasked with firing over the heads of, or through gaps in, the attacking infantry. Training for heavy machine gunners was particularly detailed, giving the individual gun commanders and the gunners exact safety margins for overhead and flank firing to avoid hitting German troops.

A high standard of map-reading skills was expected of all machine gunners in the company, but they were also expected to reconnoitre the land and, if possible, the targets before laying their guns. In an attack they would stay in their chosen position until the attack had succeeded, and then move to new, already selected, positions where they would plan their new defensive fire tasks (if staying put) or reconnoitre their next offensive fire plan.

The six mortars of the machine gun companies were 81 mm calibre, firing a 3.66 kg bomb (8 lb). The ranges were from 540–2,400 m (591–2,625 yards), with a rate of fire of 10 to 12 rounds per minute. The mortar fired high-explosive bombs and smoke. The HE bombs were particularly

effective when concentrated on enemy positions and soft-skinned vehicles in the attack, and were murderous in their effect on concentrated infantry during enemy movements and attacks.

Tactical field training

This was at the heart of all German basic training. German soldiers learned to be aggressive above all else, and were trained in aggressive movement both before the attack and during it. In defence they had an equally belligerent attitude towards the enemy. Training began once every man in the section was conversant with the use of the rifle and the light machine gun. The emphasis was always upon learning by practice, and only a few classroom periods were devoted to the real elements of the infantryman's battle skills. These skills were considered by all instructors to be best learned in the field, not at a desk.

The idea of training its men to think about what was happening on the battlefield was new. In all previous army training the emphasis had been on instant and unconditional obedience to orders, sometimes called the 'obedience of dead men' (*Kadavergehorsamkeit*), in that men merely did exactly as they were told, no more, no less. This new army was now teaching its men that if conditions warranted it, they could change their orders, or even disobey them.

Field training was designed to be as realistic as possible, and a German officer commented that 'We have considerable losses in battle training, but this is unavoidable', because 'machine guns fire ball ammunition over the heads of attacking troops, with a very small safety margin, and mortars support the infantry to within 50 yards of the objective'.

Field craft

Every soldier was trained almost incessantly by his NCOs in how to move across country. The aim of this training was to ensure that men got into battle without being killed before they could contribute to the combat. The section tactics for moving across country were only taught after each man knew how to move himself, whether in open country, woods and trees, or in a built-up area.

This posed photograph shows an MG 34 trench, with the gun loaded and the gun commander using binoculars. The man at rear has a *geballte Ladung* (a bundle of grenades) ready to throw.

On the approach march and under effective fire, German infantry moved in a series of bounds, kept as short as possible so that the enemy could not bring fire to bear on the moving men. Drills were laid down for these movements, and were also used as punishment exercises. Every man was trained in the bound method, and how to carry his weapon on the move. Machine guns were of particular importance tactically, and so gunners and their ammunition carriers had to learn how to get from one position to another without losing contact.

Equally important was learning to choose fire positions, especially for the machine gun. This was practised incessantly, day in, day out, together with using ground for concealment, how to camouflage oneself, and change camouflage when moving from one type of country to another. All was combined in constant field training exercises so that:

Tactical exercises fill half the training time. As soon as possible (within 6 weeks) new recruits are taking part in field manoeuvres that involve units as large as a division, and that includes all arms. The Germans have profited from the lessons of the First World War, when they found that half-trained troops accomplished less and sustained greater losses.

An original page from Reibert showing the form of infantry trenches for kneeling and standing men.

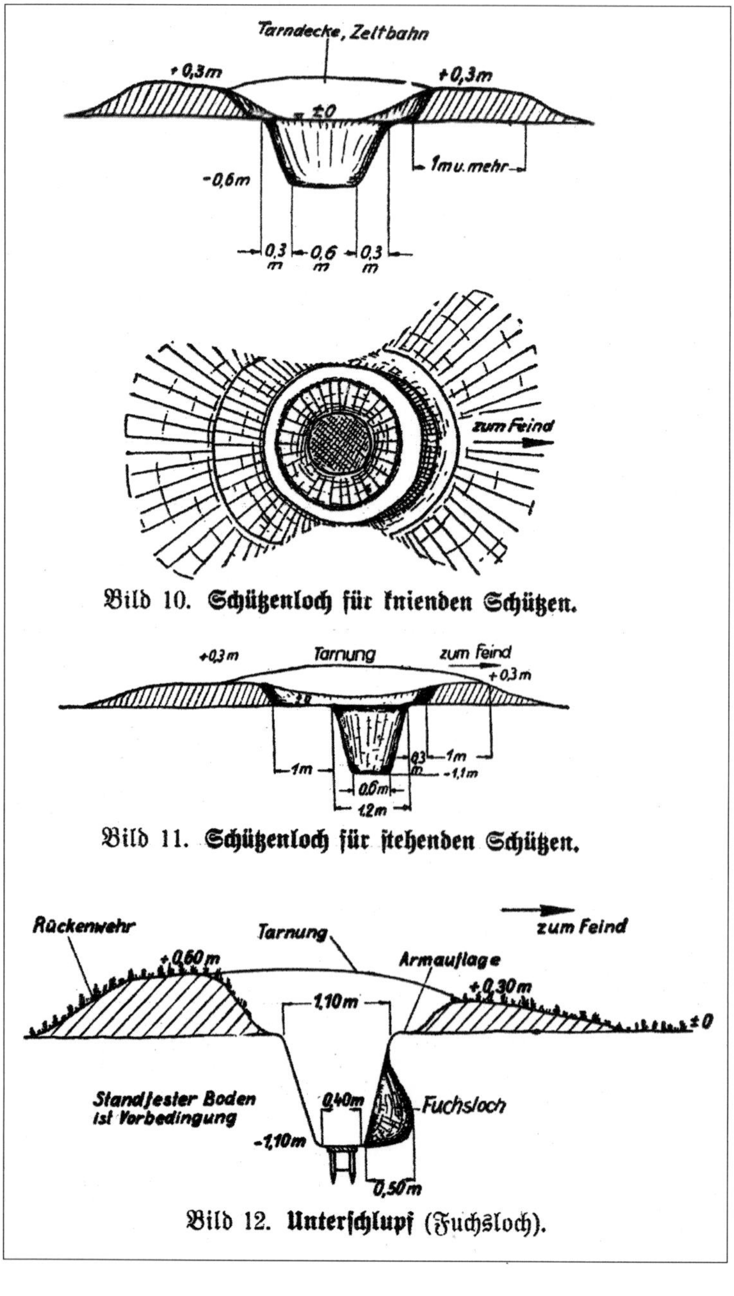

Bild 10. Schützenloch für knienden Schützen.

Bild 11. Schützenloch für stehenden Schützen.

Bild 12. Unterschlupf (Fuchsloch).

The soldier in the field has to be capable of organising himself to survive and to fight. Many hours were spent both on tactical training in field craft, and in survival on the battlefield. Not every meal could be guaranteed to come up to the front in a steaming food container. Sometimes, often frequently, the men had to cook for themselves. The Esbit personal cooker could be used to heat both food and water for coffee. Unless troops are trained in the careful use of cooking fires, they will invite retribution from artillery or aircraft for their folly. So recruits were taught to dig trenches for their fires and to make sure that the flames were fully extinguished before nightfall to avoid observation by the enemy from either ground or air.

They were also taught how to use their shelter quarter to make a waterproof coverall for themselves, and how to erect a weather shelter. This is particularly important in periods of rain or cold wind, as troops soon lose morale and fighting spirit if they cannot keep dry and relatively warm. Unfortunately for the German army no one in authority considered these requirements when the army advanced into Russia in 1941.

The German army prided itself on the ability of its men to march long distances with full loads. In training, distances and loads were increased during the first 16 weeks until by week 13 they were expected to march 28 km (17.5 miles) in full battle order and with battle ammunition issues, which added a significant 9 kg (20 lb) to their load. As they made this march they were also expected to exercise security measures front and rear and to the flank, and to carry out forward reconnaissance. Such training would stand them in good stead in the years to come. Needless to say, the route march was also used as yet another form of punishment for mistakes made in training.

ABOVE **Washing mess tins, 1938. The container in the centre of this photograph contains hot water, used to wash mess tins and mess cups.**

The tactical advance to battle

The German army emphasised the use of firepower to win the immediate fire fight with the enemy. An infantry section was considered capable of defeating a few enemy riflemen, or one machine gun. To do this, it first had to advance on foot to make contact with the enemy, either along roads or tracks, or across country, whether open or covered.

Before training began as a section in country, however, every man was practised in the various methods of getting about on the battlefield, and there was also practical training in the use of camouflage. The matter of camouflage had been brought up time and again in the 1920s by the inspectors of exercises conducted by the Reichswehr, and even von Seeckt had noted his disapproval of the somewhat casual attitude taken by the army in matters of personal camouflage. The German army was not much better at camouflage a decade later, and even in the early part of the war it was a failing noted by many observers and participants. Things really only improved when they lost their air dominance in Russia in 1942.

BELOW **This resting group in 1938 includes two riflemen, a corporal and the platoon sergeant. The effectiveness of the shelter tents ensured that troops could quickly set up bad weather protection anywhere.**

RIGHT **A platoon in battle order wearing rain capes marches along a good track in 1937, with the mounted officers of battalion headquarters behind them.**

BELOW AND NEXT PAGE
Tasks of an infantry section.

Individual role	Equipment	Tasks
All Sections		
Section Commander	Rifle Gew 98 (Wire cutters) Telescope Map case	To command and set an example to the men under his command. Responsible for: 1. Achieving battle tasks given to him and his men. 2. Controlling light machine gun fire and as the situation permits, the fire of the riflemen. 3. Maintaining the readiness and effectiveness of all weapons and equipment of the men under his command.
Section with MG O8 or MG 08/15		
Gunner 1 (Gunner)	MG 08/15, sometimes with loaded belt Pistol 08 Spare lock and container Pick Long cartridge extractor	The gunner is No 1 on the gun. Responsible for: 1. Firing the gun in battle. 2. Keeping the gun in working order at all times. 3. Care of the weapon.
Gunner 2 (Assistant Gunner)	Spare barrel and container Steam tube 1 ammunition box Spare parts container Pistol 08 Pick Gun carrying strap	No 2 on the gun in battle. When the gun is in position he lies on the left and is responsible for: 1. Keeping ammunition belts straight. 2. Assistance in setting up the gun. 3. Helping to clean the gun.
Gunner 3 (Ammunition carrier)	2 ammunition boxes Rifle Gew 98 Short spade Gun carrying strap	1. Supplying ammunition. 2. Local protection for the gun.
Gunner 4 (Runner)	Tripod Pistol 08 1 ammunition box Short spade	Responsible for: 1. Keeping contact with the section. commander. 2. Local protection.

Individual role	Equipment	Tasks
Section with MG 13		
Gunner 1 (Gunner)	MG 13 Pistol 08 Pick Tool kit for gun	As No 1 on MG 08/15
Gunner 2	Barrel holder and spare barrel 2 bandoleers with pockets for spare magazines Pistol 08 Pick Gun carrying strap	As No 2 for MG 08/15
Gunner 3	2 bandoleers with pockets for spare magazines Rifle Gew 98 Spade Gun carrying strap	As No 3 for MG 08/15
Gunner 4	Tripod Pistol 08 2 bandoleers with pockets for spare magazines Spade	As No 4 for MG 08/15
Section with MG 34		
Gunner 1 (Gunner)	MG 34 and (when loaded) ammunition belt/drum Pistol MG 34 tools container Pocket lamp/torch	As No 1 on MG 08/15
Gunner 2	Barrel holder with spare barrel 4 ammunition drums (1 loaded with A/T cartridge) 1 ammunition box or 4 drums MG carrying strap Pistol Short spade Sun glasses	As No 2 on MG 08/15. Also responsible for: 4. Reloading belts. 5. Helping to clear obstacles, change barrels and set up gun tripod.
Gunner 3	Barrel bolder with spare barrel 2 ammunition boxes MG carrying strap Rifle Kar 98k Short spade	Ammunition supply man; in battle keeps to the rear of the gun. Responsible for: 1. Replenishment of ammunition. 2. Refilling empty drums from his ammunition boxes. 3. Care of ammunition and equipment when changing gun positions. 4. Checking condition and type of ammunition to be fired by the gun. 5. Joining the rifle section when circumstances demand it.
Rifle Section		
Section 2 i/c and 5–9 Riflemen The rifle section, including the deputy section leader, assist in the fire fight with their rifles and are the section assault troops.	Rifle Kar 98k Ammunition pouches Short spade Hand grenades According to orders: MG 34 drums (especially loaded with A/T ammunition) Extra ammunition Smoke grenades Demolition charges Tripod for MG 34	The deputy section commander was responsible for: 1. Keeping the rifle section together. 2. Making sure all orders are carried out. 3. Maintaining contact with adjacent sections and the platoon commander. 4. Marking the front line (with flags carried for this).

Movement as a section

Training in movement along roads emphasised the importance of using hills and valleys, trees, stream and river beds, scrub and other natural features as cover; in built-up areas buildings filled this need. The section advanced normally (except where there was danger of the machine gun

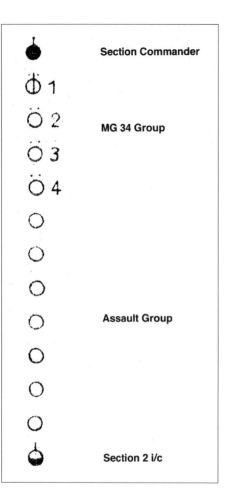

Section Commander

1

MG 34 Group

2

3

4

Assault Group

Section 2 i/c

section being destroyed) with the machine gun section following the section commander, who normally took the lead. In most cases the advance would have been made in column, with the order as in the diagram on the left.

The section was normally led by the section commander, with the machine gun group close to him. The rest of the section were spread out behind, ready to move out to either flank when they came into contact with the enemy or encountered effective fire. On the battlefield the machine gun was the centre of all infantry tactics, and the emphasis was on winning fire fights as quickly as possible, so that the riflemen of the section could assault and capture the enemy position.

Movement as a platoon and company

Once in open country and subject to enemy observation and fire, the rifle platoon advanced in open order. The diagram below shows the four-section platoon (effective from early 1940) in two forms for the advance to contact in open country. Of interest is the use of scouts (*Sicherer*), whose task was to alert the platoon (or *Gruppe*) to enemy positions, potential mine fields and other obstacles, and generally to

LEFT **A diagram of a section in the advance during the advance to contact phase of battle. As soon as contact was established with the enemy the MG 34 group would take up fire positions, with the assault group close by the initial fight was fought by the MG 34 Group.**

BELOW **The infantry platoon (section 1940) in the advance to contact. Sicherer/Scouts Gr/Section (with number); I .Gran.W.Tr /light mortar group (from *Kühlwein Schützenzug und Kompanie in Gefecht*)**

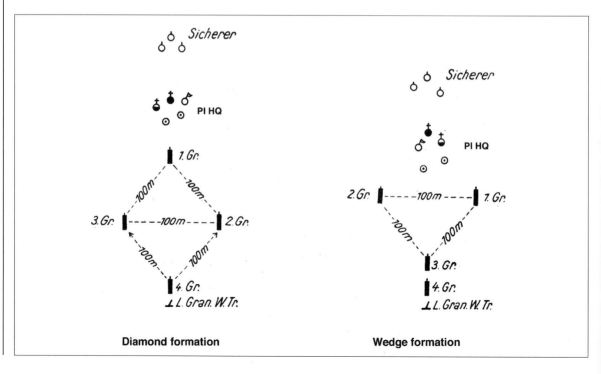

Diamond formation

Wedge formation

30

LEFT **Passing out, 1938. The battalion on parade at the end of the first 16 weeks of training. The colours of the parent regiment can just be seen in the middle of the front rank.**

BELOW **The March Past. The platoon commander salutes the Divisional General, while the platoon gives a smart 'eyes right', 1938.**

protect the leading men of the main body of the platoon from hostile action. The mortar team (*l. Gran. W. Tr.*) followed at the rear of each platoon.

It was essential that the men of the section or platoon stayed in visual, or at least audio, contact with their commander. If such contact was lost, so too was the control which is fundamentally important in battle.

The end of training

All military units love parades, and the German army was no

different. A parade was always held for the recruits when they finished their basic training, with an inspection by the divisional commander. The band played, and the successful recruits marched proudly off the square and into their future with the army.

THE CAMPAIGNS IN POLAND (1939) AND FRANCE (1940)

Hitler's decision to attack Poland in 1939 was not greeted with universal jubilation, as William Shirer noted: 'Everybody against the war. People talking openly. How can a country go into war with a population so dead against it?' One young soldier, about to depart for his regiment on the Polish border, wrote, 'I was very alarmed …'. On hearing the news at OKW Headquarters, Admiral Canaris commented, 'This means the end for Germany.'

A year later, however, when German troops entered Paris, the SS reported that this had generated 'a previously unheard of high level of morale at home and in the services generally'. (*Meldungen aus dem Reich, Vol. 4*)

This map shows the movement of 18 Infantry Division during the Polish campaign, 1939.

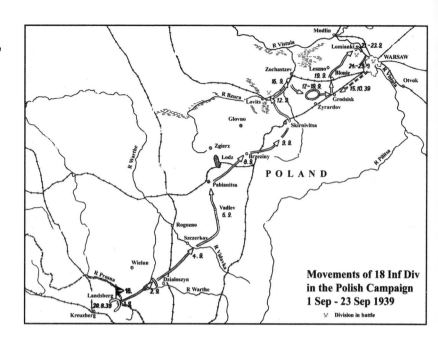

**Movements of 18 Inf Div
in the Polish Campaign
1 Sep - 23 Sep 1939**

✕ Division in battle

On the eve of war

The men of 30 Infantry Regiment had arrived in Landsberg after leaving the depot. Few Germans expected Hitler's threats to Poland to result in war, especially after the bloodless victory of the Sudetenland the previous year. However, the officers and NCOs made sure that everything that could be done was so done before H-hour ('H-hour' is a military term usually used for attack timings). The men were paraded in battle order and all their kit checked.

Machine gunners checked their weapons and ensured that the spare belts of ammunition were properly loaded into the ammunition boxes, riflemen checked their grenades and ran a pull-through along their rifle barrels. Everyone was active except the few radiomen: they had to maintain radio silence until H-hour arrived.

The night before the attack it was quite clear to everyone that this time Hitler's political gamble would not pay off: the army would be fighting the next morning. Very few men were able to sleep with the thought of battle running through their minds, particularly the perennial fear of infantrymen – wounds. This young army was 'more afraid of debilitating wounds and especially blindness than it was of death: death only happened to other people anyway.' As dawn approached the men of 30 Regiment heard aircraft overhead. The Luftwaffe had co-ordinated its arrival over the border at just the right moment, for, as the infantry moved off, they heard and saw the bombing on the horizon before them. 'Explosions from bombs dropped on Polish concentration areas sent black plumes of smoke into the sky, and we were pleased that it was our air force.' (Altenstadt)

The troops march past with weapons slung, showing that this is a unit on the way to war.

Infantryman 1933–35

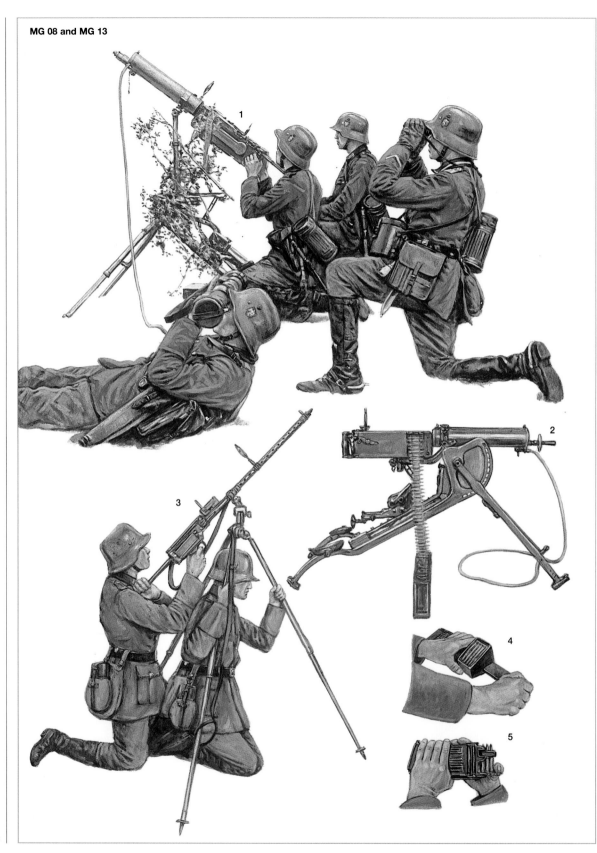

MG 34

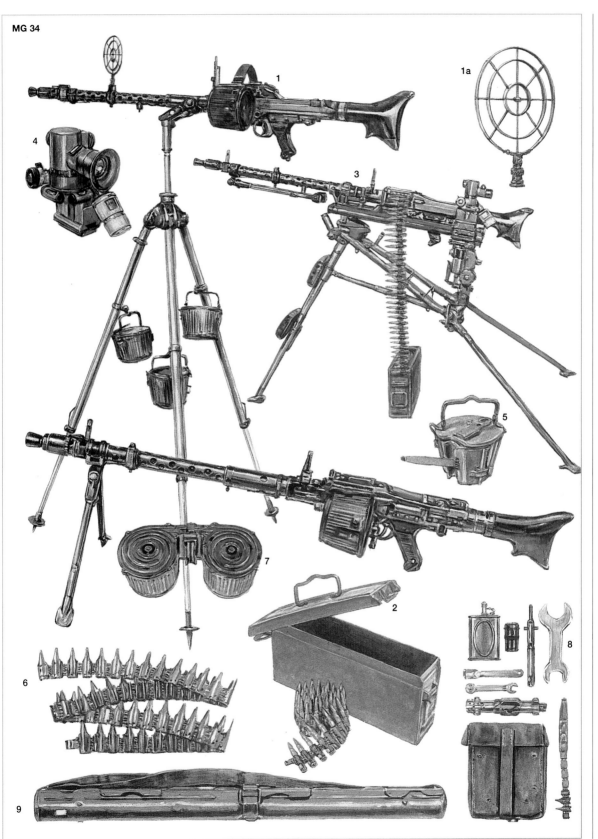

C

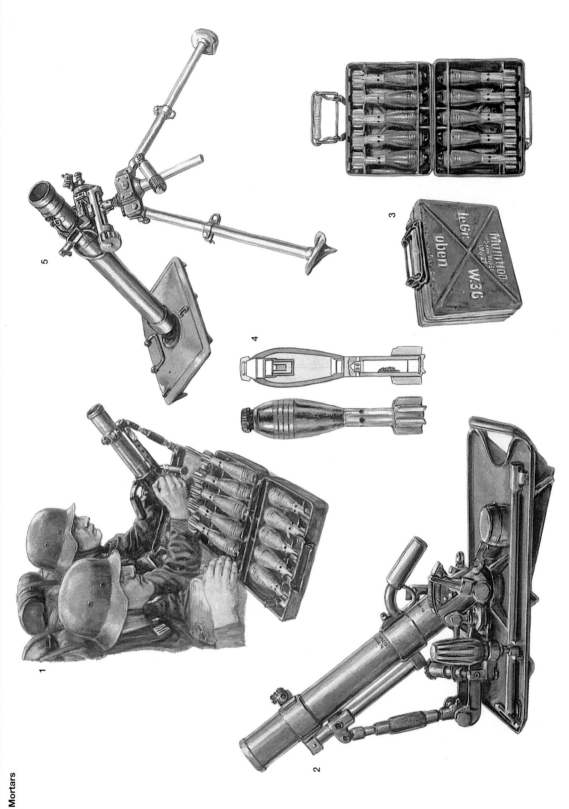

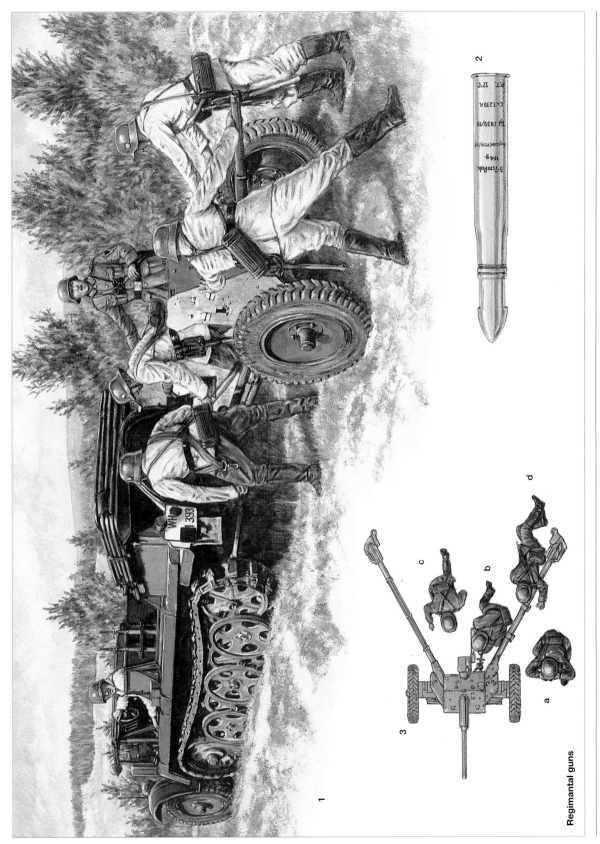

Regimantal guns

E

F

Advance to contact with enemy

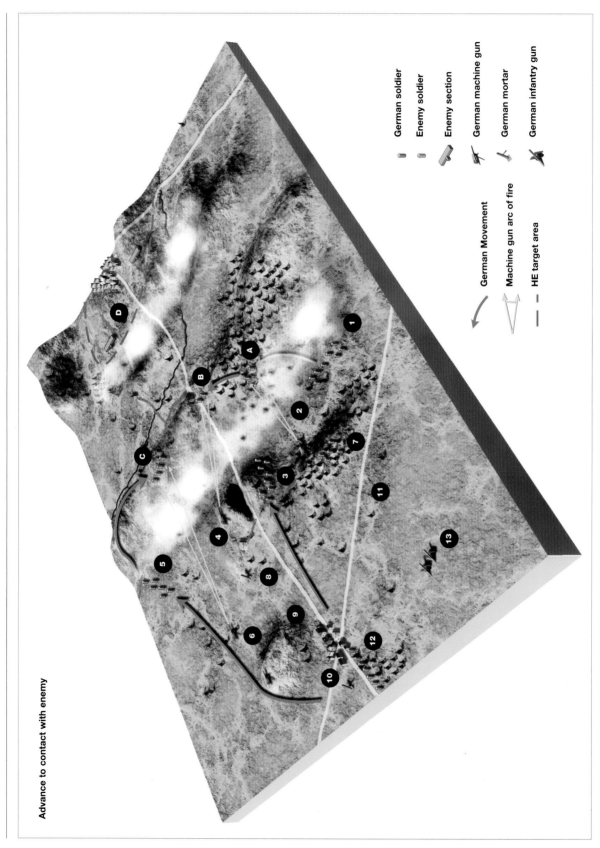

German soldier

Enemy soldier

Enemy section

German machine gun

German mortar

German infantry gun

German Movement

Machine gun arc of fire

HE target area

Fighting in built-up areas

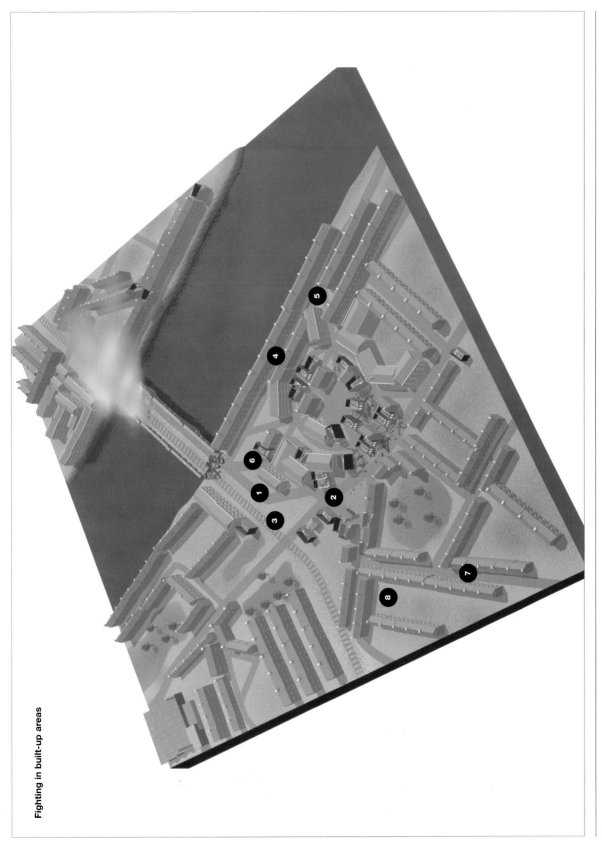

Platoon Commander, 1940

H

Marching

As the tanks and mobile infantry sped ahead, the infantrymen concentrated on their main task: much marching and some combat. Although trained to march long distances, they nevertheless became more and more tired: 'The weight of the equipment we were carrying was also a burden, one which we could not relieve. Machine gunners felt that their weapons were wearing a permanent groove in their shoulders, ammunition carriers felt their arms were getting longer, or their necks were worn raw from the carrying straps for the ammunition boxes.' Their feet began to swell with the heat, the sweat and the marching.

Only one concession had been made to the infantry of this period, which was that packs and heavier equipment were carried in horse-drawn carts which followed their platoons. The horse was still much more a part of the German army at this time, and there were very few truly motorised divisions. Most of the fighting infantry went into battle on foot, and in the whole division, only a few staff officers had cars; the only motorised units were the anti-tank gun platoons.

In France the following spring, the situation was much the same. The soldiers of 30 IR marched on, the miles soon adding up as they progressed towards west, bypassing Brussels to the south. After their experiences in Warsaw none of the men were anxious for more intensive street fighting (see below). By 16 May the regiment was over the River Dyle.

The regiment was now equipping itself with whatever wheeled transport it could find for its heavy equipment. Even children's prams were impounded to carry ammunition boxes, mortar bombs and field packs. The men found that marching demanded huge reserves of stamina, and any relief from their load was welcome. Soon civilian cars and lorries, even a fire engine, were seen advancing along the road towards Nivelles and on to Tournai.

L/Cpl. Klaus remembered:

The constant marching was beginning to tell upon us. As in Poland we were often alerted to move at around 0300, and were then on the move or in battle from then until sundown. When we crawled out of our sleeping places at first light, no-one could really believe that we had to march on yet again. The men's faces were completely blank, all emotion washed out by fatigue. But our training got the better of us, and we shouldered our weapons, picked up our packs and ammunition boxes, and went on our way. That the march was a march and not a shuffle was helped on occasions by singing, but as the days wore on the voices became weaker and fewer.

ABOVE TOP **A platoon marches in two files up to the line. The platoon commander leads, 1939.**

ABOVE BOTTOM **A platoon slogs uphill in France with its wagon and horses following.**

BELOW **Briefing. The reconnaissance platoon laid up in a bottling factory before the invasion of France started. Every means available was used to ensure the total surprise of the attack.**

Food and rest on the march

One factor which sustained the men was their food. Each company had a field kitchen attached to it, and these antiquated but essential devices were always ready, especially with the midday meal. As the battalion came to the end of the morning's march, 'every man's spirit rose at the thought of hot food and coffee. The men moved off the roads, the platoon and company wagons, plus all the accumulated transport moved into air concealment positions, and for an hour or so, things were good.' The fact that the Luftwaffe had complete air superiority helped.

Importantly, infantry platoon commanders had been trained to care for their men, and each day, as L/Cpl. Klaus recalled:

> Every platoon commander … took the opportunity to go round his platoon checking on morale, ammunition and other essentials. Weapons were inspected, and so were feet. The men's feet were swelling up from the constant marching, the heat and the dust. Socks were changed, rifles pulled through, and a cigarette or two enjoyed before, every muscle aching, the men stood up once more to face another trek until nightfall, or even beyond.

On one occasion during the campaign in France the regiment got a longer period stood-down from the advance:

> For three days the men were able to eat, sleep, tend to their cuts and bruises, clean their weapons, and sleep again. Each company had a field kitchen close to it, and with rations available, managed to feed better than they had since leaving Germany. Above all the men got their feet back into shape and rested every moment they could.

Initial combat experience

The reasonably mild weather of September 1939 meant that the troops marching east in the wake of the advancing tank divisions only saw clouds of dust ahead of them, which became more distant as the day went on. However, Polish resistance had not ended, and as they advanced they occasionally came under fire from rearguard enemy soldiers who fought bravely.

As soon as they were fired on, reconnaissance troops in the advance guard reported back to company headquarters. Following their intensive training, when the German troops were ordered into the attack they did so unhesitatingly. 'Light machine guns fired on the enemy positions – often a trench in a farm yard, or a few men behind a hedgerow – winning the fire fight. Then the assault infantry went in, and soon more Polish troops were removed from the field of battle.'

Getting a good, warm night's sleep was always high on the list of priorities, and this section has found a barn with some straw.

Up to this time the advance had been almost undisturbed, with few alarms or stops caused by the Poles. The march was seemingly never ending. They had begun their long walk on 1 September at dawn, and on 12 September had marched in the wake of the Panzer divisions, for over 150 miles. They were starting every day at dawn, and stopping only as night fell, marching all day with 20 minute breaks every two hours. The dust of the primitive roads meant constant attention to weapons was essential.

'We were fed from field kitchens at around midday, and again in the early evening: otherwise it was march, march and keep on marching. We never came up to the tanks which were very soon twenty or more miles in front of us.' (Altenstadt) Dust covered the men, mixing with their sweat to form a hard pancake on their faces and any other exposed skin. It began to cause skin problems because washing was sporadic. As the men got even more tired, so the problems were more noticeable.

In May 1940 the army went over the border to France with more confidence, having learnt valuable lessons from the campaign in Poland. 'We were off! We raced forward over the border, hoping to find bridges intact over the four rivers we had to cross on Day 1. Unfortunately each time we came in sight of the bridges, they disappeared in smoke, and the smiling Dutch engineers who had blown them up submitted cheerfully to being taken prisoners of war.' By nightfall, despite the blown bridges, they had reached their objective. They set up their shelters quickly, and wolfed down a hot meal before nightfall.

The anti-tank company, which had spent many quiet months in a small village near the Dutch border, moved to join the rest of the 18 Division on 9 May. On 10 May they were looking at

Artillery support in position before the advance over the border, 1939.

RIGHT **An MG 08 in firing position. The effect of artillery support on a Polish position just over the border can be seen in the distance. MG 08s were issued to second and lower wave divisions.**

BELOW TOP **This hitherto unseen photograph shows the first advance from the West Wall (note the 'Dragon's Teeth' tank traps in the foreground) across a marshy area, over which a corduroy road of logs has been built overnight.**

BELOW BOTTOM **Artillery support. A 15 cm sFH 36 at the edge of a wood supports the advance into France.**

the bridge over the Juliana Canal that they had hoped to capture. The infantry was working its way forward, but a few Dutch bunkers were holding them up. The anti-tank guns were quickly towed forward, and set up to fire on the enemy positions. 'The first round just caused splinters of concrete, but the next seven rounds were perfectly placed into the embrasure, and the first pill box fell silent,' remembered Cpl. Haakert. This was repeated five times before the enemy fire was stopped, and the infantry stormed across the bridge to take it. The troops started moving forward again.

For the infantrymen the night was spent either asleep, or watching their sentry sectors, for they were now in enemy territory. Men in their shelters reflected that there had been little resistance, and very few casualties, but they had a long way to go. Their next objective, and a substantial one, was the Albert Canal.

A set-piece battle

On 20 May, 11 days after the start of the French campaign, 11 Company of 30

Infantry Regiment was poised to attack Tournai and capture the south bank of the River Scheldt, but not without a fight, for the Royal Scots were present in the town. The Germans were attacking from just south of the town, and had sent out reconnaissance patrols to establish the strength and location of the British troops. 'British fire discipline was so good, that we had very little knowledge of the enemy and his locations,' noted Lt. Bergmann.

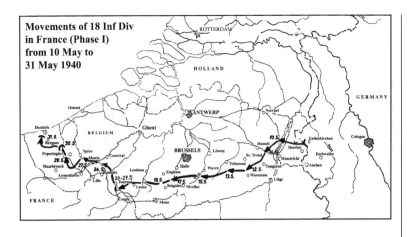

Movements of 18 Inf Div in France (Phase I) from 10 May to 31 May 1940

ABOVE **Movements of the Division during the first phase of the campaign in France in 1940.**

As the artillery barrage started, the men saw that they had to cross 600 yards to get to their objective, the bank of the river. They were ordered to attack: the company advanced from cover with one platoon leading, and two behind. They soon found themselves in a park, and had not heard a shot fired. In the middle of the park was a damaged castle. By now they were only 50 yards from the river bank, and all they could hear was the distant explosions of their own artillery support.

A wall ran round the park, and a gap in it was the objective chosen by two of the leading sections and an anti-tank gun. The river was a short distance away beyond the gap. 'Our company commander reached the hole, and stood up to observe the opposite bank; still no enemy rifle or machine gun fire had started,' recalled Lt. Bergmann. He was beginning to think that the enemy had withdrawn, as had so often happened in this campaign.

No sooner had he stood up, than all hell broke loose. The Royal Scots had held their fire, thinking that the Germans were reconnaissance troops. When they saw the anti-tank gun, however, they realised that an attack was underway, and they responded. Three machine guns opened fire on the gap in the wall, and well-aimed rifle fire began to hit the Germans, who immediately tried to find cover from this devastatingly effective fire.

Bergmann noted:

ABOVE **Cycle troops inspect a captured French field gun of First World War vintage.**

The area was now full of soldiers frantically digging in, and in between lay the wounded and the dead. The heavy machine gun team attached to the platoon managed to get to the gap and set up behind it. From that position they began to fire on the enemy machine guns, slowly reducing the effect of the enemy fire. Then came the British artillery fire, directed right on to the platoon. The anti-tank gun had already been knocked out, but now German machine guns and riflemen were being hit.

A mine has damaged the leading van, and engineer troops are searching for more mines. An anti-tank mine is being lifted in the foreground.

'The enemy artillery lengthened its range slightly, falling now behind the platoon, which allowed the 5 cm mortar and some supporting 8 cm mortars to get into action. Casualties were mounting by the minute, and there were constant calls for medical assistance from the wounded and their friends,' remembered another soldier. Enemy snipers added to the casualties, as well as more enemy machine guns. The battle raged for 18 hours before the Royal Scots were forced to move by a combination of divisional artillery and the movement of German troops elsewhere. Casualties were high on both sides.

River crossings

During the Polish campaign when the regiment finally made it to the Bzura River, they were faced for the first time with a set-piece river crossing battle. They had to cross the river against enemy opposition, and then gain and hold a bridgehead on the northern side. River crossings had formed part of their training, and once the orders were given the men prepared for the assault.

Lt. Paul Stresemann remembered this battle and wrote that 'although sick and frightened' he and his men 'ran forward with our rubber boats … with all kinds of shell fire coming at us. It was absolutely terrifying. The dust from the explosions was flying over us as we ran straight into the river … as soon as we floated into deeper water we came under terrible fire from a machine gun and the man nearest to me was killed.'

Each section in the assault party had a boat, and in the bow the machine gunner set up his weapon, pointing towards the enemy shore. The others had the task of paddling the boat across the river, a dangerous operation because their bodies were exposed to the enemy's defensive fire. However, the men were aware that the artillery would be firing high explosive on enemy positions, as well as smoke to conceal the crossing. Further support came from the Stukas of the Luftwaffe which would bomb the enemy river line before the crossing took place. A *Landser* of 18 Infantry Division, who had a slightly better experience, wrote:

As the boats of the assault wave pushed off, explosions were heard on the far bank as the artillery support fell on the Polish positions; the smoke cloud covering the crossing seemed to be working, and there were no splashes around the assault boats from enemy defensive fire. Paddling for our lives, the first wave crossed the Bzura and hit the north bank. We fled from the boats toward the top of the slight rise that was the bank itself.

As they reached the top of the bank they came clear of the smoke and saw a battlefield of explosions ahead of them. The artillery barrage moved away from them at that instant. The assault commander had fired the white signal cartridge signifying they had landed, and the signal had been relayed to the guns by the forward artillery observer on the south bank.

Now the men could see what was left of the enemy. As they stood to advance, Polish positions that had not been neutralised began firing on them. The infantry embarked on their well-rehearsed drill: locate the enemy, win the fire-fight, and make the assault. As sections, then platoons of Germans began their advance, casualties on the battlefield began to increase. 'Wounded men screaming for medical attention made themselves heard, sometimes, over the explosions of light and medium mortars, the rattle of machine guns, more distant artillery shells and the shrill of the aircraft.'

The Polish army was already demoralised, however, and the Poles knew that it was only a matter of time before the Germans reached Warsaw. Even so, they fought on gallantly, never giving up despite the

An improvised ferry for the leading troops, 1939. A rope and an assault boat provide a lift across a river. The improvised blockhouse has been knocked out, and infantry (one visible in the door shadow on the right) cover the crossing.

professional fury that the Germans unleashed on them. 30 Regiment established its bridgehead, but fought for four days before it was able to rest, near Zyrardov.

Seven months later in the West, the problem was often the canals that criss-crossed the line of advance. The regiment reached the Albert Canal on 11 May, only to find that the retreating Belgians had blown the bridge. Enemy machine gun fire was evident, and the German troops went to ground. The leading company commander decided that there had to be a fast crossing, before the enemy managed to consolidate his position, and 1 and 3 Companies were tasked with the crossing operation:

> Supporting fire was from the mortars and machine guns of the whole regiment, plus smoke and high explosive from the regiment's guns. If possible, divisional artillery support would be added, but it was out of range at that moment. Orders were given for the assault boats to be brought up quickly, and 1 and 3 Companies replenished ammunition, grenades and flares, and stocked up on iron rations in case they were isolated on the far bank.

A forward artillery officer came up to join the battalion commander, who was to be in the first wave across the canal.

Supporting fire began, and smoke bursts appeared behind the enemy, spreading as the wind blew from the northwest. As it touched the canal waters, the boats were pushed off. At the same time machine guns, mortars and even the anti-tank guns began firing on their registered targets. Their fire was not affected by the smoke, as the targets had been identified and sights set beforehand.

As on the Bzura:

> the machine gunners were in the front of the assault boats, the men behind paddling for their lives. A few men were hit whilst they were on the water, but with a speed dictated by fear, the fleet of small boats soon reached the far bank. Immediately enemy small arms fire began to have effect and incautious men were felled by the fire. The attack by the Germans was quickly organised, especially as the battalion commander had survived the crossing and was issuing orders.

'We established our first line on the top of the canal bank, and immediately started moving forward in sections, our machine guns covering the leading riflemen,' recalled Sgt. Krocker. In no time, small actions broke out as the German troops found the enemy's positions and began to attack. Incoming artillery fire was soon suppressed by orders from the forward artillery observer. The Germans quickly established their bridgehead and moved the rest of the regiment across the canal, prior to moving forward once more.

The crossing of the River Lys followed, and many casualties were incurred here, too. The Germans were nearing the end of their march, for the Channel was only 50 km (31 miles) away, but the British army stood in the gap, and they would not give up without a fight. On 26 May 10 Company was ordered to move via Zillebeke to cross the Ypres Canal

at Trois Rois. The bridges were reported intact, and the rest of the regiment was to follow. They advanced while the neighbouring battalion was under heavy artillery fire, and had reached the outskirts of Zillebeke, when German tanks and armoured personnel carriers were seen on the heights to the northwest.

'Two groups of British infantry suddenly appeared and made towards the heights, causing immense panic there, but the attack was not carried out,' reported Cpl. Dittert. Instead, the British went into Zillebeke, in the path of 10 Company. Attempts to fight through the village were defeated by machine gun and mortar fire from the British, who were fighting hard. 11 Company came up on the right just before dark, and liaised with 10 Company before both companies dug in for the night.

Interrupted by flares and machine gun fire, the night was not quiet. 'Eyes stared into the darkness until they hurt: men fired at phantoms. By dawn exhaustion was complete, and observation of the village told nothing about its enemy occupiers' remembered Cpl. Dittert. The incoming fire could not be located, and riflemen were so well concealed as to be invisible. A British mortar spent a long time irritating the Germans and was only finally knocked out by an 88 mm anti-aircraft gun.

Cpl. Dittert described more of the battle:

Relief only came with the arrival of German tanks from the northeast, but by then the company had taken on three British tanks with its anti-tank rifle and armour-piercing machine gun ammunition. It was impossible to knock the tanks out by these means, but they were turned, and they moved off. Enemy

A rifle platoon takes a break on the way to Warsaw. The man standing has two hand grenades in his boots (a common practice) and an ammunition box for an MG 34 at his feet. Note that most of the men have removed their helmets to keep a little cooler.

artillery now took up the tune, and until midday we were hard pressed to stay where we were. Trenches were deeper, but our men were still being hit.

Slowly the Germans put the advance together again, and once 10 Company had linked up with its neighbouring companies on left and right, it began its move on Ypres. 'By 27 May we had reached the war memorial, and elements of the company had got as far as the banks of the canal. By 1100 the swastika flag was raised over the towers of Ypres, where, unlike in the war before, some of the city was still intact,' reported Cpl. Dittert triumphantly.

Attacking fixed defences

Fixed defences had been built after the First World War to defend the borders of many countries, and major towns and cities were also protected by both old and new fortifications. When 18 Infantry Division got to the edge of Warsaw their first objective was a pair of forts on the outskirts of the city, Forts I and II. They were to be attacked at 0500 on 26 September, with the Field Engineering Battalion from Division in support. The plan was to attack from three sides simultaneously, crossing the moat around the forts with rubber assault boats. The engineers brought with them flamethrowers, demolition charges and the assault boats.

At 0500 the engineers dashed forward towards the moat with their assault boats, closely followed by the infantry. Covering fire from every weapon available was fired, and a smoke barrage was added for more cover. Reaching the moat the boats were quickly rowed across by both engineers and infantry, and then the assault on the gates began. Flamethrowers quickly subdued defensive fire from the reachable firing slits, and demolition charges broke down the gates. Now it was every man for himself, as the Germans flung themselves into the fort.

A French field fortification near Tournai.

The Maginot Line looked impressive, and this fort had to be well shot-up before it could be captured.

Close combat followed, with rifle, bayonet, pistol and entrenching tool all in use as weapons. Machine guns were useless in these circumstances, and had been left behind as support: here, the rifleman was at the centre of things, and with courage the Regiment slowly fought itself into the fort and to its command centre. The threat of flamethrowers and demolition charges eventually persuaded the remaining Polish soldiers to surrender, but there was a number of German bodies on the ground in and around this fort, and Fort II when it was also captured.

Fighting In Built-Up Areas

The German army had little experience or practice in Fighting In Built-Up Areas (FIBUA). 'Some of the older NCOs explained it as being similar to trench fighting, but warned that everyone had to keep their wits about them and look upwards as well as ahead – there could always be enemy positions in the upper floors, and Warsaw had a lot of high rise buildings.' Above all, they warned, do not assume that the Poles are finished; this was their capital, and they would fight.

The regiment advanced through the outskirts of Warsaw under the covering fire of medium and heavy artillery and the ubiquitous Stukas. Burning houses, rubble, wrecked vehicles and trams lay around them, and the smoke from the fires that were burning the city rose above the battlefield. The men were cautious, dashing from street corner to doorway, covering each other as they moved, always on the lookout for a

A platoon on the outskirts of Warsaw. At the tram terminus in the south some troops advance, while a few are left in the earthworks dug by the Poles for defensive purposes. By this time the campaign was all but over.

sniper or a machine gun in the upper windows of the three- and four-storey buildings they were passing.

'If fired upon, the first reaction, of diving to the ground, was useless, because men on the ground were a bigger target than standing.' They learned to return fire rapidly, and keep the enemy occupied with machine gun fire. The assault riflemen in each section then burst down the doors of the house they were attacking, either with grenades or rifle butts. A shower of grenades went in, followed by the attack into the ground floor.

'The machine gun was then brought into the building and fired through the floors and doors, whilst the riflemen grenade their way through the building. This involved close coordination and control, and those making mistakes were soon wounded or killed.' Once the building was made secure, it was on to the next corner to begin the routine again.

As they made their way through the city, there was still resistance. The Polish troops were not quitting, and often the Germans came across road blocks. Now the machine guns were not enough, and artillery could rarely be targeted so exactly, so the Germans brought up the regimental guns. Concrete bunkers were also discovered, and these had to be reduced with anti-tank guns. Often the field engineers were also called in to play their part with flamethrowers and demolition charges.

More assistance was given by the tanks of the armoured divisions, with whom, at long last, the Regiment had linked up. 'The small PzKpfw Is, with their machine guns, and the 20 mm cannon of the PzKpfw IIs were of great help in house clearing, where they gave mobile fire support, and in clearing road blocks, where the 20 mm cannon was very effective,', noted one official report. This was particularly true when the regiment reached the centre of Warsaw.

The Germans were now the victors of a 'lightning campaign', which owed as much to the initial Polish troop dispositions as to the fighting power of the German army. Indeed the greater part of the army had been involved in this campaign, against a numerically and technically inferior enemy. However, the Germans had a great success under their belts, and Hitler started to look west towards the French and British, as well as the Dutch, the Belgians and even the Norwegians.

With vital experience from Poland under their belts, the Germans turned to the west in May 1940. On 13 May, 7 Company 30 IR was preparing to attack towards the River Gette. On the right flank was 6 Company. As the men advanced in columns they came under enemy artillery fire, and were ordered to dig in. Then at 0900 'we were told to get going again and we advanced through cover towards a small village. Our nerves were screaming as we went, because we knew we were in for a dose of street fighting,' recalled Cpl. Diegardt.

Bayonets were fixed, grenades primed and stuck in their belts, and they crept forward through the last of the cover towards the enemy fire. They advanced now in short bounds until they got to the edge of the village. Each section now knew they had to have their machine gun group on one side of the street, with riflemen on the other. 'Sign language was used to order this tactical move,' remembered Cpl. Diegardt, and they started to move down the street.

'Enemy rifle fire! Everyone dashed into doorways or dived through windows for cover. Nothing could be seen of the enemy, but the fire was getting stronger.' Section commanders were now looking for the way forward, and one section saw a meadow with a useful ditch behind the house they were sheltering around. 'We moved as fast as possible across the meadow to the ditch, all the time under enemy fire. Catching our breath in the ditch, I then moved along it, towards the river, in the hope of finding out where the enemy was,' Cpl. Diegardt recollected.

Accompanied by the machine gunner, he reached a slight bend and risked raising his head. Thirty yards away were some enemy tanks, which were firing their machine guns everywhere. Then Diegardt spotted two machine gun positions. At that moment it looked as if the attack was halted, but everything changed when suddenly, the commander of 6 Company appeared in the ditch. He was quickly briefed on the situation, and sped off to arrange for an anti-tank gun to deal with the tanks.

In the next 15 minutes everything seemed to stand still for 7 Company, and the enemy fire continued unabated. Then, 'with no warning one of the tanks bounced on its tracks, and began to pour smoke from its turret. We in the ditch immediately attacked the machine gun positions, and in no time at all the rest of the company, until then held up on the edge of the village, joined the attack,' noted Cpl. Diegardt. It was soon over, and 48 prisoners were taken with four tanks and some machine guns. Surprisingly, the section from the ditch had had no casualties at all.

By the evening of 16 May, the advance guard of the regiment was approaching a small village which seemed ideal for the night. However, enemy fire broke out, and an anti-tank gun shell hit the trees above the leading men, driving wood splinters all around. 'Desperate for a night of rest, the whole regiment charged the village without orders' and the enemy were swiftly driven out. For once the men settled down under roofs and even duvets, hoping that the enemy would stay away.

Fighting against tanks

The German infantry advancing towards the Channel in 18 Infantry Division had no tanks in support for most of the time, but they were constantly aware that the enemy did, and that they were getting nearer to enemy tank country as they marched west. On 18 May the advance guard of the regiment approached the town of Ath, east of Lille. Attached to it was the anti-tank platoon, whose task was to protect the troops from enemy tanks.

The advance guard, 14 Company, reached a road leading to Ath from the south, when the sound of engines was heard. Two British tanks were soon seen, coming from the direction of the town. 'The two anti-tank guns were towed into position by the side of the road faster than had ever been done on exercises! The infantrymen were shouting 'Tanks! Tanks!" and showing signs of panic. The tanks got nearer, and their machine guns opened fire.'

S/Sgt Kiffher noted:

Infantrymen and a member of the reconnaissance company inspect a French Renault R.35 tank, knocked out in the early advance.

The first tank was fired on at about 100 yards range and the first shell broke the track, causing the tank to swerve into the ditch at the side of the road. Further shells then set it on fire, and the crew bailed out, to be captured by our jubilant infantry. The second tank continued forward, and despite being hit twice, at ranges of only twenty and then ten yards, was not stopped. It passed the two anti-tank guns, which were now in its dead zone of fire. The guns were dragged round to line up again, and this time two rounds penetrated the rear engine cover of the tank, and it too went up in flames. Once more the crew were captured, but we gunners spent a lot of time musing at the effectiveness of British tank armour.

At the same time 9 Company were also rushing forward as fast as they could, with the Regimental and Battalion commanders with the advance guard. They were aware that

The anti-tank rifle squad with their three weapons. The anti-tank rifle (The Pz.B 39) was a 7.92 mm high velocity rifle which, despite its increasing ineffectiveness, was in service throughout the war.

the town was defended, and that the bridges across the River Dendre had been blown. There was rifle and machine gun fire coming from the north bank, from where the mounted platoon had reported enemy activity. One platoon was ordered to capture the canal crossing and then take the heights to the north.

The platoon had just reached the Ath-Leuze road when engines were heard. Everyone, including the two accompanying anti-tank guns, disappeared from view. Suddenly two tanks and three motorcyclists appeared, with infantry on the tanks. 'The first tank was knocked out by an anti-tank gun, and the infantry machine gunned the crew as they dismounted for cover. A second round from the gun, at point blank range, knocked the second tank into the road ditch, but the British troops fought back, bringing a Bren gun into action,' recalled L/Cpl. Haunit.

However, the German machine guns kept the British heads down. Whilst the fire fight was going on, the Germans saw that a British soldier was in danger of being burned to death under one of the tanks. Two Germans ran to the tank and rescued the man, despite the danger of the situation. L/Cpl. Haunit witnessed the scene: 'All around was rifle and machine gun fire, exploding ammunition in the tanks, the cries of the wounded; the German fire was such that the British decided to call it a day, and they surrendered to the Germans.' Both sides were impressed by the selfless courage of the two men who had performed the rescue.

Dunkirk

The British were withdrawing concertedly to the sea port of Dunkirk, with a view to getting shipped back to England. The Germans were mostly too tired to realise that a significant victory was approaching, but most were relieved to know that it might soon be over – especially the marching. On 29 May the regiment bypassed Poperinghe, and on 31 May stood outside the city of Dunkirk itself.

The British withdrawal from Dunkirk had been going on since 28 May, and many thousands of troops had already escaped. The Germans of 30 Infantry Regiment were not privy to the debate at Supreme Headquarters as to whether tanks should go into Dunkirk, or whether the Luftwaffe should take the town (as if it could!), but they were on the eve of a mighty victory to end this phase of the campaign in France.

On 31 May the Division was ordered to replace the infantry regiment *Großdeutschland* on the La Basse-Colme Canal, to cross the canal the following day, and then to attack and capture Dunkirk. Two regiments of the division took the place of the *Großdeutschland* and prepared for the attack on 1 June. The attack went ahead, but came under heavy enfilade fire from Fort Bergues, which prevented a crossing of the canal.

The coast: members of the regiment near Dunkirk as the German advance penetrated all the defences to reach their first goal.

The regiment fought hard to stay in place and finally managed to make crossings of the flooded areas around it, although the soggy marshland 'caused more foot problems as swollen feet got wet, and flesh started to peel off', remembered Cpl. Väter. The men were nearing the end of their physical endurance, having been on the march for over 200 km (124 miles), fighting a series of engagements throughout. It soon became clear that they could not manage to take Dunkirk unless the fort at Bergues was neutralised. A Stuka attack was called in, and suddenly Fort Bergues was captured by other divisional troops. The regiment now had room to manoeuvre.

The end in the west

Dunkirk was finally taken, despite fierce resistance by the French and other Allied forces, on 4 June 1940. The division had advanced some 250 km (155 miles), and had lost 26 officers, 103 NCOs and 479 men. In addition 81 officers, 307 NCOs and 1,602 men had been wounded.

The scene on the beach at Dunkirk – German soldiers inspect the destroyed matériel left by the British in June 1940.

But the division had one more march to complete. The French had not yet capitulated, and so, to round up French stragglers and to ensure that France was totally defeated, the men had another 450 km (280 miles) on the road before they ended up in Paris. They started this third long march on 6 June and ended it on 8 July at

Corbeil, south of Paris. Light skirmishing was the order of the day, but as Cpl. Väter noted, 'many boot soles were worn through, and a lot of blisters lanced before the final day'.

Medical treatment in the field

In both campaigns, the German army had first class medical personnel and equipment to rely on in the field. Medical units attached to the infantry were horse-drawn, meaning that wound stations, casualty clearing stations, and field hospitals were close to the fighting troops, and ready to treat the wounded quickly and effectively. Just outside Dunkirk, a medical company set up their treatment centre in an undamaged school. 'As practised a hundred times and learned from experience in minor actions, the medical soldiers … brought in the equipment and set it up … As in a disturbed ant hill the Chief Doctor thought … [but] soon the confusion decreased and order prevailed.'

As the fighting intensified, 'the number of arrivals grew beyond the possibility of immediate care. The wounded men were so wet they dripped. Fighting in the flood plains beside the roads had caused the most extreme exhaustion. Lying under water, the barbed-wire fences of the cow pastures could not be seen, and the soldiers remained hanging on them in the dark, in danger of drowning and injuring themselves even more. The roadway was under the heaviest defensive fire …' To help, trained medical dogs were called in to search for the wounded, and several men were found that way. 'During this action … to care for wounded enemies, whose numbers were too great for the bandaging stations, a surgical group was detailed to the field hospital, which quickly treated some 800 wounded British soldiers simultaneously with the German wounded.'

A rifleman stands guard at a street corner in Tournai, while in the background surrendered French troops are milling around aimlessly.

A rifleman has his arm bandaged by the platoon medical orderly. These orderlies were always at risk on the battlefield, but never shirked their duty.

Reorganisation and field training

In the period between the two campaigns, 18 Infantry Division was moved back to Germany. Orders came through during this respite that platoons were to be reorganised into four sections, and an extra machine gun was issued to every platoon. The aim was to increase the fire power of the platoon, as Poland had taught the need for greater speed in winning the initial fire fight, and also the need for greater support for the assault sections.

The men of each platoon were reinforced where necessary by men from the replacement battalion at division. Revised tactics for the four-section infantry platoon and company were taught and practised interminably. Other innovations included the issue of a new canvas pack and an 'A' Frame to carry it, as well as slings to carry ammunition boxes for the light machine gun, so that the ammunition carriers could also use their rifles more easily.

The machine gun 'was found to be subject to frequent stoppages in field use, particularly in muddy or dusty areas', and development work on its successor, the MG42, was quickened. A special grenade sack was issued and every section was supposed to have a telescope-equipped rifle for small and longer range targets.

Morale was good, despite the fact that many men had been lost in Poland. For the winter of 1939–40 they were stationed near the Dutch border and told to wait. This they did, and the small patrol actions and light bombing attacks of the winter and spring caused no problems. Nor

ABOVE **A main bandaging station being set up on a pre-war exercise. These stations were the third stage of medical treatment in the German army, and were set up out of small arms range behind the front.**

LEFT **A post-capitulation exercise in France in 1940. Under cover of smoke and machine gun fire, an assault section moves out to make a right flanking attack on the farm below.**

did the tons of 'leaflets dropped during the winter of 1939–40, which were pressed into latrine duty'. (Altenstadt)

The period between the two campaigns became known as the 'Phoney War' to the British, the *Sitzkrieg* to the Germans. Many soldiers were given leave for that Christmas, although inevitably others, such as

Karl Fuchs, remained in their positions. Fuchs wrote to his mother to say, 'Our entire unit will celebrate Christmas together. Of course, we intend to buy a small Christmas tree. This will be my first Christmas in the military. Who knows how many others will follow! I guess it doesn't matter. Our duty is to defend our Fatherland.'

BIBLIOGRAPHY

The pre-1933 army is well documented in Adolf Reinicke's *Das Reichsheer 1921–1934* (1986), and the training during that period is covered to an extent by Robert M. Citino in *The Path to Blitzkrieg*, (1999). Von Seeckt and his concept of the war of manoeuvre and the air-land battle is laid out in his pamphlet, D.V.Pl.Nr.487 *Führung und Gefecht*, (1921–24) and the excellent atlas to accompany this, Major Siebert's *Atlas zu F.u.G.I.* (1928).

There is a wealth of material available on the training of the Hitlerian German army, all of which is original. The most important general books are in the series by Dr Reibert, *Der Dienstunterricht im Heer*, published annually during 1933 and 1943/4. Official manuals used include *H.Dv. 130/2a* and *2b: Ausbildungsvorschrift für die Infanterie – die Schützenkompanie* (dated variously between 1935 and 1940), *D. 130: Gebrauchsanleitung für M.G. 13 (Dreyse)*, and Butz, *M.G. 34*.

Much information is also contained in the semi-official publications of the period, many of which were used for reference and instruction by recruits and trainers alike. These include Oberleutnant Queckbörner, *Die Rekruten-Ausbildung*; Major Zimmermann, *Die neue Gruppe*; Col Kühlwein, *Schützenzug und Kompanie in Gefecht*; Lieutenant Colonel Weber, *Der Rekrut*; and Colonel von Wedel and Lieutenant Colonel Pfafferott, *Der Schütze Hilfsbuch*. Variously dated, all reprinted (and amended as necessary) at various stages between 1935 and 1943.

Further information is in Denkler, *Die Handgranate 24*, and Maj Freitag, *Infanteriegeschütz und s.Gr.W.34(8cm)*; Zeska, *Das Buch vom Heer 1940*; and Major Judeich *Jahrbuch des deutschen Heeres 1941*. Medical matters are covered in Alex Buchner, *The German Army Medical Corps in World War II* (1999), and H.Dv.59 *Unterrichtsbuch für Sanitäts-Unteroffiziere und Mannschaften* 1939.

Of the campaign in Poland there is little in the way of personal experiences, because the campaign was fought as one continuous operation for many of the participants. However, in Major Altenstadt's *Unser Weg zum Meer* (1940) there are some references to the campaign, as well as in the Department of the Army Pamphlet 20–255 (1956), *The German Campaign in Poland*, which covers the operation in some detail. Altenstadt also covers the French campaign in detail, and all references to named personnel with rank in the text are taken from this publication. One source of general, and very pertinent, information, is Stephen Fritz, *Frontsoldaten* (1995), which covers all aspects of operations and training.

Other books of use are *German Military Training* (U.S. War Department, Special Series, 1942), Donald McLean, *German Infantry Weapons* (1966), *Jane's Infantry Weapons* (1975), Major General Franke, *Handbuch der neuzeitlichen Wehrwissenschaften* (Part II, 1937), and Matthew

Cooper's *The German Army 1933–1945* (1978). The articles in *Command Magazine*'s 'Hitler's Army' (1996/2000) are of significant value, and, of course, William Schirer's *Rise and Fall of the Third Reich* cannot be omitted from any bibliography of this period in Germany's history.

The fundamental reference texts include Keilig, *Das deutsche Heer 1939–1945* (part-work); Tessin, *Verbände und Truppen der deutschen Wehemacht und Eaffen-SS 1939–1945* (1979–); Schmitz et al, *Die deutschen Divisionen 1939–1945* (1994); Schmitz/Thies, *Die Truppenkennzeichen der Verbände und Einheiten der deutschen Wehrmacht … 1939–1945* (1987). Another important secondary source is Mehner, *Die deutschen Wehrmacht 1939–1945* (1993), for officers' names, ranks and posts.

COLOUR PLATE COMMENTARY

A: INFANTRYMAN 1933–35

An infantryman in 1934 wearing the standard field jacket and trousers of the period. Belt equipment includes ammunition pouches, each holding 15 rounds of 7.92 mm ammunition for the Gew 98 in his right hand. His boots are the experimental buckled boots of 1934, which did not go into general service.

1: The German national colours, initially found on the left side of the helmet but then moved to the right when the national emblem (2) was introduced.

2: The national emblem for helmets, placed on the left side of the helmet, in white.

3: The 1916-pattern helmet with studs either side designed to allow an armour-plated brow piece to be fitted, to protect sentries in the trenches of the First World War.

4: The national emblem as applied to the uniform jacket.

5: Rank chevrons to the end of 1936: (i) senior private (*Oberschütze*); (ii) lance-corporal (*Gefreiter*); (iii) corporal (*Obergefreiter*); (iv) senior corporal (*Oberstabsgefreiter*). Sergeants' ranks were shown on their epaulets.

6: The shoulder board for an infantryman of 30 Infantry Regiment. Up to the war these were worn obviously, but as soon as operations started they were either covered with cloth or worn reversed, to conceal unit identity from the enemy.

7: Garrison cap or side hat. It was worn by soldiers in barracks and sometimes under the steel helmet to insulate the head against cold weather.

8: The Gewehr 98, the standard issue rifle of the First World War. This weapon was redesigned in the early 1930s as a shorter, more effective rifle with a turned-down bolt handle. With a calibre 7.92 mm (although known generally as 7.9 mm or 8 mm), the magazine held five rounds and it weighed over 4.3 kg (9 lb), and was sighted from 150 to 2,000 metres (164–2,187 yards). (See also 14a.)

9: The bayonet which was fixed below the muzzle of the rifle on a mounting post welded to the barrel, also shown is the black leather scabbard.

10: A five-round clip for the rifle.

11: The Pistole 08 or Luger. A 9 mm semi-automatic, it dated from before the First World War. It was superseded by the Walther P38 pistol (the holster is also seen).

12: Belt kit as seen from the rear. The upper full picture shows a rifleman in full field or marching order in 1935, with gas mask can, bayonet, entrenching tool, water bottle, bread bag and gas mask. Rolled over the pack are his greatcoat and shelter half. The detail shows how the entrenching tool was fixed to the belt.

14: The Type 24 hand grenade and a pamphlet for instruction.

14a: Pamphlets for instruction.

15: The transitional boot, with three buckles on the outside. It was soon abandoned as it was prone to let water in and was awkward in heavy undergrowth.

16: A military torch and battery. Note the coloured slides which were interchangeable.

B: MG 08 AND MG 13

1: The MG 08 water-cooled machine gun in the anti-aircraft role. The gun is mounted on the standard sled-style mounting, which has been raised to allow the gun to fire at a high angle against aircraft. The water cooling tube can be seen coming down below the gun muzzle. In the foreground is the range taker, a sergeant of the Reichswehr. The gun commander is observing through binoculars and also carries a map case, binocular case, bayonet, bread bag and gas mask container on his belt. The spurs are standard for this period (1933–34). The gunner is behind the weapon, aiming through the ring sights. An ammunition carrier is to the right of the gun.

When used in a high angle role (not shown) the sled-style mounting was extremely heavy (over 19 kg/40 lb) and the gun weighed approximately the same. During the First World War the gun was excellent in fixed positions, but extremely tiring to move on the battlefield. It was later modified to include a fixed bipod and a water jacket without pipe and reservoir. This version overheated quickly and was still too cumbersome.

2: The MG 08 in its normal role as an infantry anti-personnel weapon. During the campaign in Poland many reservists in third or fourth wave divisions were issued with this weapon, and were unable to use it, having been trained on the MG 34. The same applied to the MG 13.

3: The MG 13 was an air-cooled, magazine-fed, light machine gun. Here it is shown in the high angle role.

4: Magazine filling with a filler. Five-round clips are loaded into the box, and the slide pushes the cartridges out of their clips and straight into the MG 13 magazine.

5: Magazine filling by hand. The action is very similar to that used to load the rifle.

C: MG 34

1: The MG 34 mounted on the *Dreibein* or tripod for high angle anti-aircraft work. The ring sight (detachable) is also seen and in detail (1a).

The weapon was seen in many roles wherever the Wehrmacht went.

2: A standard ammunition box and a belt of 50 7.92 mm rounds.

3: The MG 34 mounted on its tripod for sustained fire work. Mounted like this it could be used as a heavy machine gun in the machine gun company of the infantry battalion. The gun was capable of indirect firing, and is shown fitted with the dial sight (*MG-Zieleinrichtung*). It was necessary to change the barrel every 250 rounds when in continuous action. Overheating could lead to rounds 'cooking off' or in serious cases, to barrel warping.

4: The *MG-Zieleinrichtung* dial sight. This was used to aim via indicating stakes. The gun and sight would be aimed at one of the stakes, giving a lay on a specific bearing. A correction was then set on the sight, and the gun traversed to bring the sight back on to the original stake. The gun was now laid off on the new bearing, and after elevation had been applied, the gun could fire.

5: A 75-round drum magazine and belt tab. The tab was needed to load the gun from the drum with the feed cover closed.

6: An unloaded ammunition belt. This fixed link belt could be loaded with rifle cartridges simply and quickly. The ammunition belts were sometimes joined to give a greater supply to the gun. An ammunition man would feed the rounds to the gun from a standard ammunition box.

7: The double 150-round ammunition drum. This required a special feed mechanism, but it was soon discontinued because of over-complication.

8: The MG 34 gunner's tool case and tools. Apart from spanners and a split case extractor, the case (worn on the belt) also held a spare bolt for the gun.

9: Spare barrel case.

D: MORTARS

1: The 5 cm mortar and a two-man team. The mortar is being levelled before firing. The mortar weight was 14 kg (31 lb); range 50–519 m (55–568 yds).

2: The 5 cm mortar.

3: Mortar bomb case and contents.

4: Section of an HE 5 cm mortar bomb, weighing 800 g (2 lb) with TNT filling.

5: The 8 cm infantry mortar. This was a much more effective weapon, firing a 3.5 kg (7 1b 12 oz) round out to 1,200 m (1,312 yd). Actual calibre was 81.4 mm, and the weapon weighed 57 kg (125 lb). Rate of fire: six rounds in 8–9 seconds, then 10–15 rpm. It fired HE, smoke and illumination bombs.

E: REGIMENTAL GUNS

1: An anti-tank section in training hitch their 3.7 cm PaK (Panzerabwehrkanone) 35/36 L/45 to a light tractor (Sd.Kfz.10). The crew consisted of the gun commander, the gun layer, the loader/firer, two ammunition men and the

driver of the prime mover. The gun weighed 432 kg (952 lb), making it very easy to move and manoeuvre, even by hand. It was 3.4 m long (11 ft). Barrel elevation was from –6° to +25°, with a traverse of 60°. Production began in 1928 and over 15,000 had been produced by 1941. Six of these guns were organic to every infantry regiment. Early versions had 'cart' wheels, later ones the pneumatic wheels shown here. It weighed 405 kg (892 lb horse drawn) or 515 kg (1,135 tractor-drawn); traverse was 11°, elevation –10° to +75°; maximum range was 4,600 m (or 5,030 yds) charge super, with a rate of fire of 8–12 rpm. The breech mechanism was designed on the shotgun principle, and the breech dropped to expose the gun chamber. Developed from 1927, it was first issued in 1932. The normal crew was six men, including gun commander, gun layer, loader/firer, fuse setter and two ammunition men. The gun could be manhandled in the field, although it was designed to be either horse- or tractor-drawn. The gun was also issued for mountain service as the 7.5 cm *leGebIG* (*leichtes Gebirgsinfanteriegeschütz*) 18.

2: A shell for the 3.7 cm PaK. This armour-piercing tracer shell weighed 1.5 kg (3 lb 3 oz) complete, with a projectile weight of 700 g (1 lb 8 oz). The tracer fuse was in the projectile base and ignited after 60 yards flight. The projectile was marked 3.7 cm Pak Pzgr (3.7 cm anti-tank shell). Later the gun was used to fire the tungsten cored Pzgr. 40. Muzzle velocity firing AP shot was 762 mps, and the effective range was (theoretically) 549 m (600 yds). Penetration at 30° at 100 m was 50 mm; at 500 m 36 mm. The gun fired with a shotgun-style breech action. On ejection of the fired cartridge the breech rear dropped and the casing was ejected automatically. A new round and cartridge were then loaded.

The HE shell for the 7.5 cm *leIG* (not shown), weighed 5.45 kg (12 lb). The cartridge case and charge were separate. The shell fired included HE, HE Al (an aluminium flash powder mix for observation) and a hollow charge shell for anti-tank work.

3: The gun in action. The gun commander is observing trough binoculars (a), the gun layer (b) is to the left of the breech, the loader (c) to the right. Behind them is the ammunition carrier (d).

F: ADVANCE TO CONTACT WITH THE ENEMY

This illustration shows a German infantry platoon moving to engage with the enemy. The platoon is the company advance guard, and has support weapons (medium machine guns, medium mortars and infantry guns) immediately behind it as it advances.

A, B, C and D indicate the enemy positions. A, B and C are the outpost section of an enemy platoon based around the village at D. C includes a light machine gun team.

The German platoon is advancing with three sections in line, the fourth section being at the rear. Platoon command is behind the middle section, both of which are advancing along the line of the road leading north. 1 Section advances to the right of the road, 3 section to the left. The main body of the company follows at 13.

As the centre section (3) comes through the cutting, it is subjected to effective fire from the enemy at A and B. It immediately takes up fire positions at 3, with its machine gun on the other side of the road at 4. Platoon HQ now moves to

7 and the platoon commander issues his orders as follows:

1 section will attack the enemy at A and B, supported by the section machine gun at 2.

2 section will provide fire cover and support from its positions 3 and 4 for the move and attack by 1 section.

3 section (5) will make a left flanking attack on C, with support from their section machine gun at 6.

The 5 cm mortar will fire smoke on Smoke area 1 from position 8 to cover the moves by 1 and 3 sections.

4 section (12) will remain in reserve.

A company heavy machine gun section of two guns will move to 9. If either section 1 or 3 fires a red signal flare, launch fire support for them on to their target. They will then move to C on completion of this assault.

A medium mortar section will fire smoke from position 10 on Smoke target 1.

Regimental artillery (2 guns) will fire from position 11. The guns will fire HE on enemy area D.

After completion 1 and 3 sections will stay where they are, and platoon HQ, all machine guns and the 5 cm mortar will move up to enemy area B–C in preparation for the company attack on enemy area D. Support weapons will join.

The German combination of infantry machine guns, mortars and artillery, available so quickly after contact, was one of the main reasons for their success in the attack in the early part of the war. The weight of fire would force the enemy to keep his head down, allowing the attacking infantry (at 1, 3 and 5) to make their moves and their final assault. The Germans believed that overwhelming fire superiority was the key to infantry operations; it was for this reason that so many machine guns were provided. Smoke was used prolifically to very good tactical effect.

G: FIGHTING IN BUILT-UP AREAS

The map shows infantry operations in Warsaw east of the Danzig station. The east end of the bridge is the stop line, agreed between the Germans and the Russians.

1: A 3.7 cm Pak takes on a Polish armoured car in front of the west road block on the bridge and destroys it.

2: An MG 34 team covers the rear of the infantry at (3) and (6) and is ready to move up to (1) when ordered.

3: Infantry and a PzKpfw I wait for orders to advance towards the bridge. They will advance through (1) in coordination with the infantry at (6), making sure both sides of the road are covered by infantry and armour supporting fire.

4: Another 3.7 cm Pak fires on the west road block from the river embankment, backed by a PzKpfw I at (5).

6: The second assault group follow an armoured car which is firing on the west road block.

7: Reinforcements approach the battle zone pushing their bicycles.

8: An 8 cm infantry mortar fires smoke onto the bridge to obscure German movements from the east road block and the Polish machine gun position on the east bank.

9: Heavy field artillery fires further support onto the east bank of the river on and around the east road block.

The attack will concentrate on the west road block first, and infantry and armour will destroy that objective. The next move is across the bridge under covering fire with smoke to destroy the east road block. The move across the bridge will be made by infantry using tanks as cover.

H: PLATOON COMMANDER, 1940

1: The platoon commander carries an MP38 and a magazine case for three magazines on his belt, as well as his map case.

2: Wire cutters.

3: Minefield marker flags.

4: German army torch. Many were issued, but men sometimes bought their own. The red filter was useful for night work, as it affected night sight to a much lesser degree.

5a/5b: The MP 38 submachine gun in section and from the left side. An effective weapon at short ranges, it suffered from exposure to dust, mud and constant rain. The weapon weighed 4.1 kg (9 lb), and had a rate of fire of 500 rpm.

6: Issue binoculars. These had a plain lens with a graticule for range estimation and for calculating lead when firing at moving targets.

7: Issue march compass and case. Carried by section commanders, platoon sergeants and commanders and used for direction maintenance on the march, and for fire orders for indirect fire by medium machine guns, mortars and artillery.

8: The Walther 9 mm P38, which replaced the Luger as the standard pistol of the German army in 1940.

9: The Walther signal pistol and cartridges. The pistol was 2.7 cm calibre, and widely issued as light signals were frequent, especially white flares to show where German troops were. Cartridges emitted white, red, yellow, green and blue flares.

10: The magazine loading tool for MP 38 magazines which loaded individual cartridges into the magazine.

11: A leather three-magazine pouch for the MP 38. Often two were worn, one of which had a small pocket for (10).

12: Three MP 38 magazines. Each magazine held 32 rounds of 9 mm parabellum cartridges, with a muzzle velocity of 390 mps.

13: An officer's map case. Inside were maps, with pockets for pencils and markers. This could be worn on belt loops, or on a sling around the neck.

14: Standard army issue whistle. Used to signal start orders to troops.

INDEX

Figures in **bold** refer to illustrations